Writing at University

Third Edition

Writing at University

A guide for students

Third Edition

Phyllis Creme and Mary R. Lea

 Open University Press

Open University Press
McGraw-Hill Education
McGraw-Hill House
Shoppenhangers Road
Maidenhead
Berkshire
England
SL6 2QL

email: enquiries@openup.co.uk
world wide web: www.openup.co.uk

and Two Penn Plaza, New York, NY 10121-2289, USA

First published 2008

A catalogue record of this book is available from the British Library

ISBN-13: 978 0 335 22116 5 (pb)
ISBN-10: 0 335 22116 5 (pb)

Library of Congress Cataloguing-in-Publication Data
CIP data applied for

Typeset by RefineCatch Limited, Bungay, Suffolk
Printed and bound by CPI Group (UK) Ltd, Croydon, CR0 4YY

Fictitious names of companies, products, people, characters and/or
data that may be used herein (in case studies or in examples) are not
intended to represent any real individual, company, product or event.

The *McGraw·Hill* Companies

This book is dedicated to our parents:
For Beryl Lea and in memory of Howard Lea
In memory of Joan Butler and John Power

Contents

Acknowledgements

The first edition

The material in this book is based on both research and practice that we have been involved in over the last few years. It would be impossible to acknowledge every source from which we have developed our ideas about university writing, but there are those that do require specific mention. The quotes from students are based on what has been said to us over the years in various university settings, where we have worked with, and researched on, students and their writing. The quotes from staff in Chapter 3 were based on interview data collected during work carried out for the Teaching and Curriculum Development Services at the University of Kent, UK. Research by Mary Lea and Professor Brian Street (Perspectives on Academic Literacies: An Institutional Approach), funded by the Economic and Social Research Council, was particularly influential in our thinking. Some materials collected during this and other research – for example, student essays, handouts and course information – have formed the basis for some of our examples. It seemed inappropriate to reference these directly because they were not 'published material' and additionally they had all been made available for students. We hope that if members of academic staff should identify too closely with particular assignment questions they will accept our use of them in good faith as exemplars.

We would like to thank colleagues and students involved in writing workshops, and other staff, at the University of North London.

There are some individuals who have made their own particular contributions. We are grateful to Martha Radice for her piece on mind maps and to Hannah Knox for her example of note taking and her mind map. Thank you also to Hannah for her useful comments on some of the chapters. We thank Charles Knox for his illustrations. We cannot name all the students who have contributed by giving us their understandings of writing assignments but without them this book would never have been written. We would also like to thank our families for their support, particularly in the last stages of putting it all together.

Lastly, writing this book has been a collaborative project in which we have had to merge ways of writing from our own different disciplinary backgrounds. We have not always found this easy and so we would like to acknowledge each other for being supportive at the times when, for one or other of us, confidence in the writing process was lacking.

The second edition

Nearly six years after this book was first published we are revising it in order to take account of some recent changes. Students are now finding themselves having to do many different kinds of writing at university. At the same time, the use of new technologies is becoming commonplace. Chapter 10 explores both of these issues. On many courses students are asked to reflect on and evaluate their own learning, and the use of learning journals is becoming frequent. We have therefore ended this new edition with Chapter 11 on the uses of 'exploratory' writing, which extends the emphasis throughout the book on the relationship between writing and learning.

We would like to acknowledge the contributions of students and tutors at the University of Sussex to Phyllis Creme's research on the uses of 'New Forms of Writing and Assessment', and subsequent work on writing for learning. This research was initially funded by the Higher Education Funding Council for England (HEFCE) and the National Network for Teaching and Learning Anthropology 1997–8. Particular thanks go to Jane Cowan, Ann Whitehead, Jeff Pratt, William Locke and Neill Thew. We are grateful to Alys Conran, Madeline Knox and Emily Towers for allowing us to use examples of their work. As always the authors would like to acknowledge each other's encouragement and the support of Shona Mullen at Open University Press.

The third edition

In this third edition we have reorganized some parts of the book and have taken account of both reviewers' feedback on the second edition and current concerns and interests in the field. We therefore include more detailed considerations of plagiarism and further exploration of making an argument. In considering argument in Chapter 7, we foreground the dialogic nature of writing. In Chapter 8, we explore plagiarism against the backdrop of a more general discussion about the use of sources.

Phyllis Creme would like to thank Teryn Evans, for her essay on Socrates in Chapter 7, Suzanne Beeke and the PhD students on the UCL Writing and Learning Mentor Programme for their contributions to discussions about argument. We are grateful to Adrian Chapman, Anne McGee, Colleen McKenna, Sally Mitchell, Stephen Rowland and many others for stimulating debates and discussions. We also thank those reviewers who took the trouble to comment on our previous edition and to give us ideas for this one.

Finally, this edition is the product of our collaboration as colleagues and friends over more than a decade, and many fruitful conversations have helped both of us to deepen our understanding of student writing.

1

You and university writing

Why a book on university writing? • Working with others • You as a writer • Different types of writing • Talking for writing • Getting started, keeping going and dealing with writing blocks • Getting help • A note on word processing • A tour through the rest of the book

I never understand what they want.

Writing here seems completely different to anything I've done before.

The thought of writing assignments just makes me panic.

This book is about writing university assignments at degree level. Some parts will also be relevant to students taking postgraduate courses who are new to an area of study. One of the main reasons why we decided to write this book was that we wanted to help students find ways of putting writing at the centre of their learning. We believe that writing for your studies and learning for your studies are so integrally related that they cannot be separated from each other. Obviously an important aim for you as a student is that you complete your written assignments on time and get good grades, but writing essays and other assignments is about more than that: it is fundamentally about learning. As you learn to write in a particular way for a particular subject you are learning how to make sense of that subject. Academic disciplines have their own ways of organizing knowledge, and the ways in which people in different subject areas write about their subjects are actually part of the subject itself and something that has to be learnt. This is something that we will return to later in the book.

As authors we obviously do not know the readers of this book, nor how they came to be at university, but we do know that there have been many changes in universities during the last decade and that not everybody makes a simple and smooth progression from school after achieving the required A-level grades. There are now many routes into higher education and it is increasingly common for students to have had a variety of different learning experiences, both good and bad, before deciding to embark on a university course. Therefore, it is quite likely that you have been used to both learning and writing in many different ways. Now, at university, you will be asked to complete written assignments which not only seem very different from each other but also appear to have very different criteria for assessment. We hope that by working through the strategies and tasks suggested in this book you will become familiar with ways of working that will enable you to tackle a range of different writing for university.

1.1 Why a book on university writing?

There is a common belief that writing is writing and that, if you are taught the basics, you are either good at it or you are not; that either you can do it or you cannot. We disagree with this point of view. So why is it that some students seem to find it so easy to complete their written work while others seem to struggle? From our own experience of working with university students we believe that the key to becoming a successful writer at university level is understanding what is required and what is involved in the process of completing assignments. Once you have grasped what it is that you are meant to be doing, writing tasks become much more straightforward. Our own work has helped us become aware of how complex writing university assignments actually is, and we wanted to write something for students which helped them to understand this. This book is designed to help you to think of yourself as a writer, and to understand the ways in which you may need to adapt what you already know and do in writing, to the writing that you have to complete at university level. Whether you are just starting your course or are still wondering about it all after a while, then working through this book should help you clarify matters and tackle your assignments more confidently.

You may be surprised that, apart from a section in Chapter 11, there does not seem to be very much about grammar and punctuation. You may think that these are the main difficulties that you have with your writing. You may even have picked up this book because you have been told by your tutor that you have writing problems and that therefore you need to improve your grammar and sentence structure. Just because we don't deal with these issues very much directly until a later chapter does not mean that we do not think that they are important, but we do believe that writing involves much more than a working knowledge of the formal structures of written English. We feel that if you learn to work on your writing in the ways that we suggest and through the tasks that we introduce, it will become much easier for you to attend to the more formal issues of grammar and punctuation.

In your university assignments you will usually be expected to use standard English, formal written English, the language of education and other public institutions. For many students this can seem an 'unnatural' form, but these formal structures should become much easier to grasp and apply as you become used to a wider range of reading as well as writing. One good way of increasing your own command of standard English is to read articles in the broadsheet newspapers. Articles about issues are more useful in this respect than reading the reported stories. In general, reading is a very good way of broadening your own knowledge of different forms of writing as well as being essential for writing your university assignments. In this book we will help you to identify different ways of approaching reading materials and how you can incorporate them into your writing.

Chapters 2 to 11 take you right through the work of preparing and completing your university assignment. Although this book is designed to be worked through from the beginning to the end, and the tasks and strategies we use do build one upon the other, it is also the kind of book that you can dip into if you are having particular difficulties with a piece of written work. However, we would encourage you to try some of the tasks at the beginning as they form the basis for what comes later. The book does not just consist of these tasks; we also illustrate how to develop your own understanding of what it is that you are supposed to be doing when writing for university. We don't pretend it is easy but we do believe that you can work on, improve and develop your own writing. Writing for university need not be a mystery.

1.2 Working with others

Although this book is addressed to the individual reader, we want to emphasize the value of working with others on your writing. Sometimes at university you will have the opportunity of joining a study skills or writing development group, or will get some practice or guidance in the kinds of writing you have to do within your courses, but often you are left to work this out for yourself. It is true that a large part of writing is a solitary activity, an aspect that some people value but others find difficult, especially if you are used to working with others most of the time. However, there are many parts of the writing process where it is enormously useful to get ideas and feedback from others. Many professional academic writers make use of a 'critical friend' to read drafts or talk though ideas.

On some of your courses you may be asked to produce a group report or other piece of writing. Your group will have to work out how to do this and how to get as much benefit as possible from using the different resources of the group. Even when you are working on your own it is very useful to look at someone else's assignments after they have been completed. We would suggest that you try to find ways of working with other students on a range of aspects of your studying, including writing. For instance, you could form a structured self-help group or work less formally with a friend. This is not cheating! There will still remain the central core of the writing that has to be done on your own. We are not suggesting that you co-write an assignment (although there may be occasions when this is appropriate), just that you find a critical reader to explore and perhaps provide feedback on what you may be doing. A few of the tasks in the following chapters specifically need to be done with someone else, but it would also be beneficial to work through the book as a whole collaboratively.

1.3 You as a writer

How do you think of yourself as a writer? You may feel more or less confident about writing, but whatever your background, whether you have come straight from school, whether you left formal education many years ago, whether you have completed an access or foundation course, whether you are from a professional background or are studying purely for personal interest later in life, you will have already experienced many different forms of writing. At university level, writing can seem strange and unfamiliar. Even for those who have recently done A levels, the requirements can be very different from what they are used to. Puzzling over the assignment title in front of you, gathering your thoughts and ideas together, and incorporating what you have read about the subject into your work, can feel pretty daunting. Rest assured, this does not only apply to first-year students – even hardened academics feel like this when they are writing articles for learned journals.

The first activity in the book asks you to think about the way in which you have used language before coming to the university; this is in order to help you to think consciously about the experience you have to build on as you tackle university writing. Focusing on the different types of writing that you have experienced, and what each one entails, helps you to think more clearly about university writing and how it is similar to, or contrasts with, other types of writing that you have been used to. This activity is not only about writing but also about using language in general; it is important to remember that writing is just one particular way of using language, and that your other language experiences are also important influences on how you write.

Activity One: Writing your own linguistic history

Think, and write down as much as you can, about your own personal linguistic history, the ways in which you have written, read and spoken in your life. Here are some questions to help you to think about this:

- Think back to your childhood and what sorts of writing you had to do. What were the writing tasks at school? Did you write for other purposes?
- Did you find writing easy or were there some things that you found particularly difficult? Do you know why?
- What sorts of reading have you done over the years and what have you enjoyed?
- Have you ever kept a diary or written poetry, a short story or a novel?
- Do you regularly write letters, emails, text messages?
- Have you had to write reports, minutes or formal letters in your work?
- Thinking more generally, how did people speak around you when you were growing up? Can you remember different ways of speaking in different circumstances, for example at school or home?
- Do you, or did you, speak more than one language? If so can you think of any things that you find difficult to say in one language and easier in another?

Now read through what you have written and think about the different kinds of writing that you have done in your life. Write down the ways in which you think essay and assignment writing differs from, or is similar to, other kinds of writing.

Think about:

- The purpose – why are you writing?
- The audience – who are you writing for?
- The types of writing – how would you describe the writing?

1.4 Different types of writing

In some ways we can see all writing as being the same. Writing consists of words and these words are put together in particular formations to make sentences. Sentences are then grouped together into paragraphs. However, even at this point things begin to get tricky if we think of all writing as being the same. It is quite possible to communicate what we need to say in writing with an incomplete sentence. A good example of this would be a note left for maybe a partner or a work colleague:

Dinner in the oven

Three copies please, asap

As long as they were in the know, and the context was familiar, people would easily understand these simple messages, but they do not consist of complete sentences. Neither phrase contains a main verb. If we wanted to turn these into formal standard English we would have to say something like:

Your dinner is in the oven.

Please would you make three photocopies of this article as soon as you can.

In these examples 'is' and 'make' are the main verbs of the sentences. Of course when we are writing a quick note to somebody we can still express ourselves clearly despite the fact that words are omitted. One of the reasons for this is that as writers we can reasonably assume that the reader will understand what we are trying to communicate by leaving the note. When we write letters or emails to friends we often use a rather informal chatty style and leave out words because the meaning is still communicated clearly. In fact, if we wrote to our friends in formal standard English it could sound quite cold and unfriendly. However, in other circumstances we use language in more formal ways, resulting in different types of writing.

As you work through this book you will see that we emphasize that, as in the rest of life, at university there is more than one way of writing. Your writing will have different purposes and functions, although university assignments are mainly produced to inform your tutors and lecturers about your knowledge and understanding of the subject area. You will find that you can communicate with your reader, the tutor, through various types of written assignment depending on the discipline and subject areas that you are studying.

1.5 Talking for writing

We have said already that working with others can help you to develop and enjoy your writing. There is another reason for working with others, whether as part of your course contact time or in a self-help group, or just informally with a friend: talking about ideas and material from the subjects you are studying is always a good way of learning the subject. It allows you to state something boldly, even if you are unsure about whether it is 'right' or indeed really what you think, and then you can expand and modify it as you get other people's reactions. In talking around a subject you can also raise and explore your own questions, clarify your understanding and discover a variety of other ways of seeing a topic. Talking can help you to develop your writing. For example, tutors sometimes report that when they are giving verbal feedback to a student the student will say 'What I really meant was this . . .' and the tutor says 'Well, that's not what you put in your essay'. The advantage of a tutorial, or any face-to-face contact with your lecturers, is that it gives you the opportunity to ask questions and clear up misunderstandings. If the tutor does not understand you in a seminar then you can always say the same thing in a different way, but when you are writing an assignment you have to let the reader know exactly what you mean through your writing. This is often extremely difficult, particularly as many people find that speaking an idea is generally much easier than writing it.

The following activity should help you to explore, for yourself, the relationship between speaking and writing. You will need to work with a fellow student to help you with this activity and you will need to record your conversation. This activity will be useful practice for drawing on discussions and other 'course-related talk' for your writing.

Activity Two: Speaking and writing

Work in pairs. Think about an assignment that you are having difficulty with at the moment.

Record yourself (for no more than ten minutes) having a conversation with your friend about the problems that you are having with this piece of work.

When you have finished, both of you should take a blank piece of paper, and without listening to the recording again write about the things that came out in your conversation.

Discuss your writing with your friend. Do you both think that it really reflects what you said?

Listen to the recording again. Is what you have written a fair reflection of the conversation? Has writing it down changed what you now think about what you said?

1.6 Getting started, keeping going and dealing with writing blocks

I always put off the assignment until the last minute. I simply don't give myself enough time to do a good piece of work.

I just sit there; I can't write anything. My ideas just don't come.

When I am writing my mind just keeps wandering – I can't keep up my concentration.

At this early stage it might be useful for you to anticipate some difficulties with starting and getting on with writing that students frequently experience. Writers traditionally find writing difficult. There is something about the 'blank sheet of paper' that can induce panic. It may make you question whether you can possibly have anything to say that is worthwhile. You may be asking how you can bridge the gap between what is in your head and a complete piece of writing. Most students find getting started on an assignment difficult at some point. They may have spent a long time reading and thinking, and feel that they cannot transform this into a manageable plan for an assignment. If they have tried to make a plan, the step of actually writing might stall them. They may come to a full stop after writing for a while – or think that perhaps they should start the whole assignment again in a different way, when there is no time left.

There are many reasons for finding writing difficult, but probably a fundamental one is lack of confidence and feeling that you don't have anything to say. Almost every writer, experienced as well as inexperienced, seems to face this sometimes. Every new piece of writing seems to be a new challenge. If you can accept this you might find it easier to cope. In Activity One we asked you to think about some of the ways in which you had been used to writing. It is possible that you have been used to a particular type of writing which means that you feel rather blocked when you first approach unfamiliar university assignments. This was the experience of one student who had held a senior position in the health service: she was used to writing comprehensive and detailed reports for management committees but still experienced a writing block when she began her degree. You may simply need more of a sense of method and practice, and many of the activities in this book are designed to help you achieve this. Try to accept yourself as a writer and acknowledge that getting started is a common problem. Think of being a student in a professional way. You might find studying either more satisfying or more daunting than work you are used to, and you might be expected to carry it out more independently; this is all the more reason for treating writing assignments like a job of work. Writing for university is not something you can just expect to come easily but nor should it involve so much of yourself that it is really daunting. In the end you simply have to do it as well as you can, accepting that, like any other activity, you will get better as you go along. Accept, too, that everybody works differently.

As you get more experienced you will gradually build up confidence in your own methods and approaches to writing. Always remember that having difficulty with writing does not reflect on you as a person or on your general ability to study. Put effort into your assignment but accept that it might be criticized (and tutors are not always expert at being tactful in these matters). Try to learn from their comments and accept that they are not criticizing you as a person or as a student. Remember that writing is fundamentally a way of learning as well as a way of producing an assignment for assessment. Some of your struggle with writing and getting started will be the result of tackling new material in new ways, as part of the learning process, so that even if you have difficulties with your actual writing it does not mean that you are not making progress with your learning.

It is also important to accept that the 'rhythm of writing' varies rather unpredictably. Sometimes you seem to be achieving a lot, sometimes very little. Sometimes, if you keep going even when you don't seem to be achieving much, suddenly you can have a breakthrough and it becomes easier again. If today everything seems to be slow, tomorrow the benefits of your hard work will show, and you find you can achieve a lot in a very short time. Develop realistic strategies, for example about what reading you are able to do in the time available. Make time for initial planning and for the final stages of redrafting and editing your work, as well as for the writing. There are many parts of writing assignments that you can do in smallish bits but for writing the whole thing you really need an uninterrupted period of time.

Keeping a learning log

- Keep a notebook to write down interesting ideas connected with your courses, from lectures, reading, talking and thinking.
- What questions or thoughts did a session raise for you?
- What was interesting for you?

Although we suggest that you should see writing as something like a job of work, try also to think of ways of making it enjoyable. Working with other students can be really encouraging. You might also want to think of ways of playing around with writing, for instance, brainstorming or making diagrams or mind maps to get down your ideas; there are examples of these throughout the book. What is more, we should emphasize that despite – or perhaps because of – the difficulties, learning to express and develop your ideas in writing can be satisfying and rewarding. A student who comes to think of herself or himself as a writer at university can feel like a new person.

1.7 Getting help

Try to talk about any difficulties with other students or your subject tutor, particularly if there is something that is course-related that you are finding difficult. It is most unlikely that your difficulties are unique. You may have the opportunity to seek help from a study support service in your university.

Problems with writing may be associated with other problems. If you still have difficulty in getting started and feel really blocked with your writing, you may find it useful to discuss the problem with a student counsellor, who will understand and who is trained to help.

1.8 A note on word processing

Word processing has dramatically changed the way many people write. For example, first thoughts can look – misleadingly – as though they are in a finished state, and the ability to change what you write as you go makes revising a very different process from writing out many drafts. Here is one student's experience:

> Since I have been at university I have incorporated word processing into the method I use for writing my essays. I make notes on the reading and construct an essay plan on paper and then move on to the computer to start writing the essay. I find it useful to write an introductory paragraph directly on to the computer as I think that the beginning is one of the hardest parts. Typing it on the computer forces me to start and lets me get into the flow of the essay without worrying too much about what I have written. I usually go back and change it into a coherent introduction at the end. Nevertheless, I feel I need to have something at the beginning so that I can get a feel for the essay before I embark on the main body of the assignment.
>
> I normally print out what I have written when I am about halfway through so that I can read it properly and make changes by hand. I can then think through what I am going to write in the second half and how I will relate it to what I have already written. When I have finished the essay, written the references and done a spell check, I print it again to read it through as I find it difficult to read the essay as a whole when it is on the screen. Sometimes there are still typing errors or parts which don't link together very well so I change these by hand on the printed copy, then on the computer, and when I am satisfied I hand it in.

1.9 A tour through the rest of the book

As we have already said, this book is designed for you to choose the different sections and activities that seem the most relevant for you, but we do recommend that you read it all the way through to get a complete picture of writing at university.

Chapter 2 introduces some important ways of getting started and approaching university writing for the first time. It is a good idea to familiarize yourself with, and practise, the techniques covered as they will be useful for you to use later on in your studies.

In Chapter 3 we consider what it means to write for different courses. Most students find that they are being asked to write in a number of different ways during their time at university. This chapter should help you to identify the different course requirements that you will encounter for writing assignments.

Chapter 4 focuses on the importance of analysing the assignment title and addressing the question set. The activities in this chapter are designed for you to apply to any written assignment that you come across while at university.

Chapter 5 looks at reading as an integral part of the writing process and directs you to useful strategies that you can adopt when reading for your assignments. You will also be encouraged to think about yourself as a reader of your own work.

In Chapter 6 we introduce different approaches to planning, shaping and organizing your writing. Activities help you to think about your own planning process and how to find your central idea.

Chapter 7 takes up the subject of developing an argument and how to persuade, and how to take your reader into account in your writing.

Chapter 8 looks at how to draw on and cite different sources in your assignment writing. It also invites you to think about what plagiarism means in academic writing and how to use your sources so that you can avoid it.

Chapter 9 addresses a question that puzzles many students: how do I get myself into this assignment? It looks at different ways of writing academic knowledge and how to move from the personal to the academic. It also suggests strategies for using the first person and writing your own opinions.

By the time you get to Chapter 10 you will be concerned with putting everything together and editing and redrafting your work. These issues are dealt with here, in addition to approaches to writing introductions and conclusions.

Chapter 11 looks at the overall sense of your written text and how to make it coherent. Some attention is given to punctuation as one way of making sure that your writing will make sense to the reader. The chapter also suggests ways of building on the feedback that you will get from your tutor.

In Chapter 12 we explore how you could tackle different kinds of writing that you might have to do at university in addition to essays. We also look at issues of writing online.

Chapter 13 looks at learning journals and reflective writing, which help you to take a more personal approach to your learning and deepen your understanding.

Just a final note. This book is about writing for assignments and does not make any direct reference to writing for exams. However, we believe that developing your understanding and experience, through attending to the tasks and strategies in this book, should help you to tackle any of your writing that has to be undertaken under exam conditions.

Notes

- It is important to practise different kinds of writing. Try to build up the sense that for most university courses writing is a crucial element and that part of your work as a student is to write.
- Don't confine your writing to the required assignments. Try to turn yourself into a regular writer who does a bit of some kind of writing every day.
- Take every opportunity to take part in seminars and discussion groups, and try to set up a self-help group to discuss reading and related activities and to review assignments.
- Use the activities in the following chapters as ways of building up your range of writing and reading techniques, and remind yourself that at each stage of preparing an assignment you know more than you think.
- Keep a learning log.

2

Getting started

*Bridging a gap: you and university study • Practice writing •
Brainstorming • Generating questions*

It all seems like another planet.

*It's like learning a new language – you have to start from the beginning
again.*

I just don't know where to begin.

In this chapter we will assume that you are about to begin your university
study (whether in an area which is new to you or not) and are asking questions
about what you will have to do for writing at university. We will explore
what is involved in university writing and will suggest some first steps that you
can take towards tackling your assignments. Our aim is to help you to be
confident in starting out; our message in this chapter is that you need to be
courageous, prepared to take risks, and committed enough to keep practising.
We acknowledge that university writing can be difficult but believe that there
are ways of approaching it that will build up your confidence and develop your
competence. This chapter uses three well-known methods for beginning to
write: *practice writing* (based on a commonly used 'freewriting' technique
developed by Peter Elbow) to get started with the writing; *brainstorming* to get
down as many ideas as you can as quickly as you can; *generating your own
questions* to think around a topic.

We will suggest that you try out these techniques in different ways and for
different purposes, both for getting information and ideas, and for presenting
them. The tasks are all designed to help you to get started quickly, so that you

can use what you already know, and find ways of extending and developing your thinking. We hope that you will enjoy trying these ideas, which are about thinking, working and writing confidently.

2.1 Bridging a gap: you and university study

When you come to write at university you may find that there is a gap that you have to bridge. On one side there is you, with your background, sense of identity and ideas about the world, and on the other there is the subject you have to write about, based on academic disciplines. It can seem like a foreign country, far away from you and your familiar setting. This new place can open up interesting new ways of seeing and understanding for you but it can also present problems of how to behave, and how to speak and write. It is rather like joining a group of people involved in a particular activity, who have been talking together for some time. You have to feel your way into what the group is talking about: they seem to share ideas that they don't even mention, and you don't seem to be able to take part in the way they use language. If you do join in you may be saying something that doesn't fit with what else is said. You don't know if they may have discussed it already. In any case, you can't find the right words and you expect to be met with silence and puzzlement and to look foolish. However, usually after listening for a while, once you do start to take part you can adjust to what is going on and start to contribute in your own way. You feel awkward at first but if you don't mind this, it gets easier. The more you take part the more you are bridging the gap between what you came with and a different way of thinking and speaking. It can feel the same way with your university writing.

In higher education different ways of thinking and understanding the world are expressed through the different academic disciplines, the broad subject areas that are the basis of university study. Disciplines – for example, physics, history, psychology – have traditionally been the ways in which a body of people have made sense of and 'represented' the world: that is, built up particular ways of talking about the aspects of the world that their discipline looks at and explores. You will often find reference to 'academic communities', which have even been called 'academic tribes' to indicate how they have different customs and territorial claims. The conventions and ways of viewing and representing the world of different disciplines are often not made explicit to students. Sometimes academics can be so engrossed in their subject that they seem to forget that they need to explain their discipline, as a particular way of constructing knowledge about the world, to students. You may therefore find yourself struggling to find out both what you can say and how you can say it when you write for university. We take up this issue again in Chapter 9. As a student you will find yourself going backwards and forwards between different disciplines, and we say more about this and ways of writing for different courses in Chapters 3 and 12.

An example of the 'foreignness' of university study that you may encounter immediately is that subjects have their own jargon – words and terms that are used in a specific way in their own context. Even if you look them up in the dictionary, you still won't understand the way they are used in a particular subject area because their contextual meanings are specific and unusual. Familiar words are used differently and new terms are invented. Different uses of words indicate different ways of thinking about and viewing the world, so it is important that you learn the new terms and meanings and that you are able to use them in your writing. The next activity will help you with this.

Activity Three: Make a glossary of terms

Take any subject that you are studying. Choose a few terms that are commonly used in it. Use your own words to try to pin down what the term means for you. If you are noting words that are already familiar to you, think about where your present understanding of them comes from.

As you continue your study, note down where and how the terms come up and how they are used; you may want to collect and note actual examples of their usage. Adjust your definitions accordingly. In some cases introductory texts or a specialist subject dictionary will give you guidance on the meaning of terms but there is really no substitute for becoming familiar with how they are used in context, and learning to use them yourself in your own writing.

Pay attention to unfamiliar terms in the extracts and main body of *this* book as you work through it. Use your computer to put together a glossary of terms, editing it as you learn more about the terms you have included. Print it off regularly so that you can use the hard copy for reference.

2.2 Practice writing

When you are first trying to get into the method of a new kind of writing it can be very useful to make yourself try to write as much as you can about a topic, as a way of getting your ideas into some kind of external form, and in the process discovering what these ideas are. Since you are simply practising writing at this stage, we call this 'practice writing'. The essential idea of this method is that it doesn't matter what the writing is like because the only reader, unless you choose otherwise, will be yourself. It doesn't matter whether it is well written, or even whether it makes sense; the point is to keep doing it. You keep writing, in continuous prose, not notes, and try to write as much as you can, either in a preset time or for as long as you can go on. The point is that it doesn't matter what or how you write – just that you practise doing it.

The idea of practising writing for university may not seem very controversial but in fact most students don't do much ongoing writing for their courses – instead they just have to produce assignments each term as finished products. It isn't usually suggested that they may need to do a lot of preliminary practice of small amounts of different kinds of writing. Yet it is obvious that to be a tennis player you have to practise. It is the same with university writing: just as learning the rules of tennis isn't the same as being able to play, neither is reading about a subject the way to learn to write about it – although of course reading is an essential prerequisite for university writing.

One thing that makes writing difficult is that we are inclined to be critical of what we are writing as we do it and to try to make the writing good and correct from the beginning. This habit may come from experiences at school. If you are writing something that you find easy, where you know more or less what you want to say, this may work, and you might possibly end up with a piece of writing that you can use straight away. This is very rare, however. In doing a piece of writing for university, you have to accept that you will be likely to need several attempts, correcting and amending it, to get it right; you will need to redraft and edit your writing. We look at this process in Chapter 10. An important purpose of practice writing is that it separates the first thinking part of writing from the critical editing part. Trying to get your writing right in every way can inhibit you from allowing your ideas to flow freely and your language to develop. The message is simple: you can't be expected to do everything at once. In practice writing you are rigorously turning your back on your editing voice which tells you that this isn't making sense, suggests that you go back and start again, or, even worse, insinuates that this is so terrible there is no point in trying and you'll never be able to do it. With practice writing you are doing one thing at a time and discovering what you know, in the way you yourself can express it, right from the beginning.

Practice writing is an easy way of making yourself do plenty of writing. However, as you proceed you will want to make it more focused. Try the technique, for example, when you have had a lecture. If you are able to take five minutes at the end to practice-write about it, without referring to your notes, you may be surprised at how much you can remember and produce, and how effectively you will be getting down ideas from the lecture which you can make good use of later.

In the following activity on practice writing, we suggest a topic, 'The family', because we go on to discuss this as an example. If you prefer, try it now on a topic that is more closely connected to your study. Notice that here we are suggesting that you work on a general topic from your course, whereas later in the book we examine assignments in a more focused way.

Activity Four: Practice writing for university

Set a timer for five minutes, then just write as much as you can on 'The family in Britain today'. Start from any point of view you like. You may, for instance, find it easier to start with your experience of your own family. Remember that it doesn't matter where you start or what you write because this is writing for practice and to get you started. Write in continuous prose, not just notes.

When you have finished, read through what you have written. What do you think of it?

Identify what you have written about and think about why.

Notice how you have written. Do you pursue one thought or jump about? Have you written in complete sentences?

Did this exercise work for you? Are there any surprises in what you have done?

Keep this writing by you as you work through the next few pages on the family.

You may be surprised at what you have written. (Writers are often surprised at what they write.) You may have kept to one idea or have written in a more random way. Perhaps you find that you are enjoying playing with ideas or language. Even if you have not written very coherently, you will notice that it makes some sort of sense, although you may not have bothered much with punctuation. You may like this piece of writing, and might want to develop it.

Here is an example of an attempt at this task:

The family in Britain today
Families are fine when they work but they don't work very well often, sometimes they even get what social scientists call dysfunctional, what does this mean? Well it seems to mean that none of them can get on with each other and they can't work like families should. All families have their problems but I think that is a part of being in a family, so what do we mean by a family anyway? I think that this is changing all the time and if we go to other cultures we see how different families are. My great grand-mother was one of 17 children and all her uncles and aunts lived in one town, but my family lives all over the place and mostly we don't see each other beyond the immediate ones. Lots of my friends live in different kinds of families like with just their mum or dad or with other people and I live with my half-brother so it's difficult to see what a family might mean in the future. Anyway I enjoyed seeing some of my family last Christmas but again in America it's thanksgiving for families.

You see that this writer has many thoughts about families but they are rather jumbled up and her punctuation and grammar are imprecise. She is not 'editing' as she writes. The piece reads more like speech than formal writing, as if she is talking to herself – which indeed she is. It is noticeable that the writer uses her own personal outlook to think about families in more general terms. She is getting her ideas from her own experiences and probably from the media, where general ideas and opinions about the family are often expressed. However, she also uses the term 'dysfunctional' to refer to families that are not functioning in ways that they might be expected to. This is not originally an everyday term but has become adopted into more general use. If this writer were to continue with her writing at this stage her ideas would probably begin to flow more easily and the connections would be clearer. As we see in Chapter 6, some writers find that writing like this is a good way to start a piece of work. Once they have gathered information, practice writing is a way of getting down what they know as quickly as they can, so that they can begin to look at what they have in front of them and from that plan their assignment.

The term 'family' has a very wide range of meanings and associations. Your own thinking and your talk about 'my family' may be determined mainly by your personal and social background and experiences. The family is also a topical public issue, and the media and politicians have a good deal to say about it, from different perspectives, in ways that are charged with conflicting meanings that represent the interests and views of different groups. For example, the term 'family values' has different associations for different groups, some positive, some negative. Academic disciplines speak about the family in specific ways which have different meanings from those of politicians, the law, the church and the media. The following list indicates different kinds of approaches of different disciplines:

- **Sociology**: how the family functions as a group or fits into the larger structure of society. How the concept of the family is used to explain social issues.
- **Psychology**: the impact of family relationships on the individual.
- **Literary studies**: how fiction depicts a particular family and how this relates to the language and form of a novel.
- **History**: how family patterns and behaviour have changed over time.
- **Social anthropology**: families in different cultures, with different cultural interpretations of the meanings of the family.
- **Biology**: 'family' used as a category or a means of classification – a group of objects distinguished by common features.

To give a fuller example, here are two attempts to deal with the idea of the family at the beginning of a sociology essay:

> The word 'family' can mean different things . . . in this country, when social policy makers refer to the family, they commonly mean the 'nuclear family', involving two parents and their children.

The traditional notion of the family with the father as breadwinner in the public sphere of paid employment and mother as carer in the private world of home is increasingly remote from the reality of modern day households . . .

You will notice that these writers are concerned with different ideas about what the family means rather than offering any set definition. One of the important aspects of university study is that it can invite us to question our currently held assumptions and ideas; so that, for example, you can come to compare what 'the family' has meant to you with how your understanding changes from studying it as a part of a university course.

Fast writing

There are many other ways of using short bursts of writing to explore course ideas and your own learning. Here are some suggestions for 'fast writing' and you may like to think of others for yourself during your studies.

- Keep an 'ideas' notebook for noting down ideas as they occur to you. Many academics, including your tutors, do this. You might find it especially useful if you are engaged in a project or a dissertation.
- Write a 'note to yourself' about what you might want to say in a seminar or other kind of discussion. You can do this during the seminar itself.
- Send an email to fellow students about your thoughts on a lecture or other learning activity.
- Brainstorm ideas for an assignment, then choose some that seem important and try 'practice writing' about each in turn for a few minutes. In each case keep on writing, and write in sentences not notes.
- Generally, try to build up a sense of yourself as someone who uses writing regularly as part of your studying.

2.3 Brainstorming

The next method that we look at for getting started on an assignment uses note form rather than the continuous prose of practice writing. The idea of brainstorming your ideas is that you simply note down as many ideas as possible about a topic, in words or phrases. As with practice writing, it is important that you don't censor what you come up with; just note down anything you can, as quickly as possible. Later you will select and throw out some items. You can do this task as a list, but many people like to begin to arrange their brainstorming ideas spatially, which helps them to see how they relate to each other. It can therefore be a good idea to use a blank piece of A4 paper so that you can arrange your jottings where you like over the page as you think of them.

As in the practice writing exercise, use your own topic for the following activity if you prefer.

Activity Five: Brainstorm for writing

Take the topic 'The family in Britain today'. Write down as many points about this topic as you can, using single words or phrases. You may find it useful to arrange your ideas spatially on your page, to give you an idea of how they begin to group together.

Now compare the brainstorming ideas that you have noted with the list below. Can you think about where your own ideas have come from?

The family in Britain today

- Parents – parenting – should it be taught?
- Different cultures – different models of what is a family.
- Families are difficult and can be completely dysfunctional.
- Is the nuclear family on its way out? Ideal family in 'ads'.
- New kinds of family emerging – e.g. shared parenting, civil partnerships.
- High rate of divorce.
- Family Christmas – do I want it?
- Family values – meaning – use by politicians.
- Are families in decline?

Even from as small a list as this you will see that this writer has a number of ideas about different and changing family patterns that she might want to pursue in further study. It shows that she has ideas which she will be able to draw on, for example in a social studies course. Studying on a university course will give her the opportunity to clarify, systematize and change her thinking. This list seems to come from the writer's thinking on what she has read in the media, a kind of 'general knowledge' that she has picked up and that would be shared by many people from the same culture. Perhaps the same is true for you, or you might have ideas from your personal or work experience. The relationship between what you already have in mind and your study will be variable but it is a good idea to begin by clarifying and exploring any ideas that you already have. Once you have done this you will need to get your ideas more organized and focused on particular questions and assignment titles. You may also use the brainstorming method as a way of pushing your thinking further as well as for beginning to organize your ideas.

Some students like doing this kind of brainstorming thinking by using a 'spider diagram' (see Figure 2.1). The basis for this technique, which has now become very familiar, and which you may know, is that ideas are not arranged in our heads in a simple linear structure, one following another, but in different patterns. To force ideas into a linear sequence, as writing prose does, from a beginning to an end, is to give a kind of structure to our mental constructs that does not really fit them as they are. You see how in Figure 2.1 the notes can be put in different places right from the start, and then links between different ideas can be added as the writer considers them. You can experiment with different ways of representing your ideas visually.

2.4 Generating questions

At this point we will move to the first stages in thinking about producing a specific assignment, as one way of getting used to the process. In Chapter 4 we will give you a more systematic method for tackling a particular assignment. Let us take a possible question from a first-year politics course as an example. We don't necessarily expect you to know anything about the topic below from the point of view of a university politics course. The point of this task is to define your own thoughts as a preliminary to further work. In order to model the process for yourself, we suggest that you try out the following activity from your general knowledge and understanding. Then, in the future, you should be able to apply this method to one of your own assignments.

Activity Six: Generate questions on a topic

Work on this title: 'What is racism? Can it be eradicated?' Make a list of as many questions as you can that this title suggests to you. You are not, of course, expected to answer any of these questions – just to pose them.
   Now compare your list with the following example:

- What do we mean by race?
- What are the causes of racism?
- Is racism mainly to do with black and white?
- Is racism an innate human characteristic?
- Are there some societies where racism doesn't exist?
- Are there different kinds of racism?
- How has racism manifested itself historically?
- Can anyone be racist?
- What is the connection between racism and religious intolerance?
- What effect have laws against racism had?
- Is policy-making and the law an answer?
- How am I personally affected by racism?
- Is there a difference between racism and prejudice?

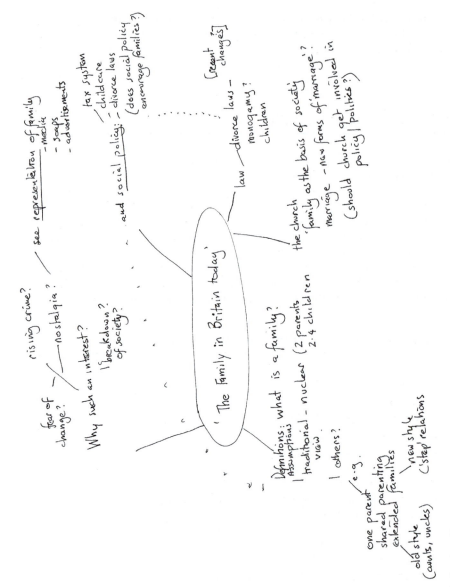

Figure 2.1 Spider diagram

These questions are very varied and you will realize that neither this assignment nor even a fairly general politics course could answer all of them. They certainly do not begin to form a plan for an essay. It is also interesting that all of these questions could lead to further questioning, which, as we explore further in Chapter 4, is an important part of being able to be searching and analytical in your writing. It is always important that the student as well as the tutor asks questions. Generate questions for yourself when you embark on a new course, and as you are about to read a book or article, or attend a lecture. Formulating the questions helps you to be clear about how you conceive the subject and what you hope you will get from the materials and other sources of information. It starts you thinking in a purposeful way as you explore different sources for ideas.

As you embark on your study you can expect to encounter various ways in which you will be helped towards tackling assignment questions. Firstly, your course syllabus or handbook should give you a good idea about how the particular topic of your chosen assignment fits into others. Lecturers may also suggest appropriate ways in which you might think about the topics. Handouts may direct you to particular readings, or provide a series of different definitions. In discussion groups of various kinds you may be asked to introduce particular topics. This will give you the opportunity to explore your own understanding in the company of others who do not necessarily share your views. You may find that you have to defend your opinions, or listen to others and change what you think on how you approach a topic. In all of this it is always a good idea to do your own thinking first, to put together and make concrete your ideas, see how they relate to what you are learning at university, and develop them by more thinking and reading.

Course handouts may:

Define what you have to learn.

Provide material that is especially relevant for the particular course.

Provide definitions and explanations; work notes; follow-up questions.

Lectures may:

Define the range of the course of study.

Process a wide range of information into a form that you, the student, can handle more easily.

Give you a model of how to practise the subject.

Seminars/discussion groups (including online) may:

Give you the chance to talk about the subject and practise using its language.

Enable you to explore and develop your ideas in company with others.

Require you to give presentations on an aspect of the subject of study.

In this chapter we have been looking at ways of getting started with your university writing. The process of thinking and rethinking that you should be going through in your studying will be easier and more productive if you keep formulating and processing your ideas in a range of different kinds of writing. If you make sure that this includes a good deal of continuous prose, you will build up a sense of your own identity as a university writer.

Notes

- Look out for new terminology and, if necessary, ask the meaning of terms in different subjects. Notice unfamiliar terms in this book.
- Use brainstorming to clarify what you know and what you think before you start any new piece of work.
- Practise many different kinds of writing as much as you can and don't just rely on writing assignments.
- Don't expect that you can get your writing right the first time you do it. Remember that writing is for learning.
- Be prepared to think broadly before you focus in on a question or a particular assignment.

3

Writing for different courses

Ways of writing • Different perspectives • Unpacking assignments • Key elements of university writing • Different ways of knowing • Structure and argument • The traditional essay format approach to writing • The 'building blocks' approach to writing

The thing I've learnt now on this course is that it's all about for or against, and criticizing one argument with another.

In management science students are encouraged to include examples from their own experience and are less oriented towards textbook theory than other subjects.

This year I've done courses from English, drama and Spanish and the writing is completely different for all of them.

One of the most difficult things to learn about being a university student is how to tackle the variety of different written assignments that you will be asked to complete throughout the course. Normally, when we think of writing at university we think about 'how to write an essay'. In fact, traditional essay writing may be only one of many types of writing that you will come across during your studies. You may be asked to write reports or to write about your subject area from a particular point of view, for example in a journalistic style or for a professional audience. You may be required to write a summary, an evaluation of a piece of personal research, a commentary or a critique of a book or article (see Chapter 12). In this chapter we will be thinking about some of the different types of writing that students have been asked to do and hope to get you thinking about the writing that you have come across at university so far. Different types of writing require different approaches. Before you can adequately complete a piece of written work you have to find ways of unpacking what that particular piece of work is likely to entail.

3.1 Ways of writing

If you are writing in a way with which you are familiar, you will be able to go through this unpacking process without even thinking about it. We talked about this in Chapter 1. A good example of this is to think about letter writing. Most of us send letters at some time in our lives. If you write a letter to a friend then you are likely to find that writing it comes quite easily to you. However, if you had to write a letter of condolence to the same friend then you would probably find yourself having to think very carefully, not just about the wording but about what you wanted to communicate in the writing. It is very likely that you would be aware of the possible responses that your friend would be likely to have to reading your letter. In contrast, you may at times have to write a letter for a job application, a letter of complaint to the local council or to your bank manager to ask for an overdraft. Each type of writing would be different but it is not very easy to identify why each is different from the other, or more importantly what new strategies you are adopting as you begin to write. When we write we are – often subconsciously – thinking about our audience; we draw from an enormous lexicon of words to express what it is that we wish to communicate to the person, real or imagined, who is going to read what we have written. Sometimes the 'ground rules' of what to write seem very clear and explicit. In other circumstances we find ourselves floundering around trying to work out what might be appropriate ways of writing.

3.2 Different perspectives

Writing in different ways and for different purposes does not just involve using different vocabulary. It is about the way that ideas are ordered into sentences and paragraphs to communicate to the reader of each particular piece of writing. At university the way that we write about something is determined by the assignment title within the discipline or subject that we are studying. One useful way of thinking about the different writing requirements of our courses is to think in terms of 'fields of study' rather than disciplines or subjects. The traditional academic disciplines are much less clearly defined than they were in the past, and so it is difficult to say specifically how you are expected to write in, for example, history, English or psychology. The way that you will be expected to write depends very much upon the particular orientation of the course and what degree programme you are following. For example, you may find yourself studying issues concerning the environment from a geographical, social, cultural or biological perspective, depending upon the particular course or unit that you are undertaking. The way in which you will be expected to write about environmental issues depends not on the subject area, 'environmental studies', but on the specific orientation of the course and the academic staff who designed it. In a similar way, a student in her first term at university was asked to complete the following written assignments, which were all being taken within an English degree programme:

- Provide a semiotic analysis of a visual image of your own choice, explaining possible denotational and connotational meanings, and showing how specific features of the image contribute to these meanings.
- Write an essay of about 1500 words reviewing a current London production in the light of the perspectives offered by the unit.
- Write a detailed account of your reading of one of the poems from the anthology, showing how that reading is influenced by one of the following: your race; your class; your gender; your education.
- Choose one novel which you have studied in the unit and, making use of one or two secondary critical texts, offer a critical discussion of ways in which the novel of your choice has been read by another critic.

Although they were all assignments from English-based courses, the student had to approach each piece of writing in a different way, drawing on different kinds of source material and different types of analysis for her final writing. In the first, she was required to analyse an image (possibly an advertisement), and, therefore, in her writing it was necessary to take on some new and complex vocabulary, and to use this to move back and forth between the image and her interpretation of it. (We talked about using new terminology in Chapter 2.) In the second, although she was directed to write an essay, she actually had to write something more akin to a theatre review. In the third case, she found herself having to incorporate some of her own experiences into her writing, whereas in the last assignment, although she was able to make her own choice of novel, the emphasis was on the secondary sources from other authors which would inform her analysis. Each piece of writing was asking her to look at the area of knowledge – the visual image, the play, the poem and the novel – in a particular way and from a particular perspective.

3.3 Unpacking assignments

As a student you have to learn how to unpack what may be required in each new assignment. It is unlikely that the requirements of any piece of writing will be clearly spelt out to you; in fact a major part of learning to study at university is finding ways of understanding how to write your knowledge within a particular 'field of study' for a particular audience – in most cases the tutor who is going to mark your work. Each time you come across a new way of writing your knowledge in a particular 'field of study' it can seem strangely unfamiliar and very difficult to work out. Part of learning about that 'field of study' is learning to write it in your assignments. That is why it is very important that you try to work out what is involved in writing any particular piece of work. One way of doing this is to ask your tutor or the person who set your assignment. Most tutors will themselves be trained in a particular discipline and they are often expecting and looking for particular ways of writing that disciplinary knowledge within the 'field of study'.

The quotes from tutors below show some of the ways in which tutors in higher education have described their disciplines and what they are looking for in their students' written work. It is important to remember that these are individual tutors talking about what they see as necessary in a good piece of student writing. *We are not describing specific, definitive ways of writing these particular disciplines.* The purpose of these quotes is to help you to see that you, the student, are often being asked to write in many different ways as you move from one written assignment to another.

Students come into my course from many different backgrounds – sociology, anthropology, psychology, history, philosophy, American studies – and because of this they often have a lot of problems with their writing. Basically, I am looking for a traditional essay format and am particularly concerned with getting students to tease out the logic of an argument and look at the relationship between premises and conclusions. I often find that students under-analyse things and that their own voices are not heard in their writing. Writing essays is all about different strategies of interpretation and students find this difficult. In one of the courses I teach some of the students from social science subjects are very inexperienced at using the personal in their writing. Some of the students from English or history do not really know how to interpret the particular texts we use in this course in their writing.

(Politics tutor)

The students who are doing courses from the humanities in conjunction with this course seem to have some difficulties with their essays. In their other courses tutors are looking for spontaneity, personal reactions and something original. Those who come from social sciences write in a more organized but rather conventional way; they are better at developing an argument and using data to illustrate the argument. I am looking for something else again but I am not looking for a fixed style. Basically, the style of writing should be related to what students are saying. Adopting a personal perspective can be useful in essays but it is never more than a take-off point, and is something to incorporate into the main body of the essay from other materials that they have read. Your own experience can illustrate interesting points but cannot possibly do more than that. Some students keep intervening in terms of their own personal likes and dislikes and find it difficult to distance themselves from their own opinions. This is not really acceptable but students can give an anecdotal example to help bring out a point, particularly if it fits in with other examples and can show that this illustrates the point that they are trying to make. In this way they can incorporate the personal. An increasing tendency is for students to write safe essays based on basic facts. A good essay has to have structure and content and be well argued but apart from that there are not any strict guidelines about how to write an assignment. By the final year I would expect my students' writing to be about processing information, not just the facts.

(Social anthropology tutor)

Some students tend to 'copy' rather than express themselves in their writing. Law requires information processing and analytic skills and students have difficulties with using their legal knowledge to work through the argument to a legal solution. Sometimes we use sample answers which deal with the substance of a legal point; the sample answer deals with the substance of the legal point but not with issues of style and presentation. In student writing the use of correct terminology is very important – for example, in civil law you cannot say X is guilty, you must say X is liable. This sort of thing is very important for students to get right in their writing. In critical legal studies students are not just learning but evaluating and deconstructing many of their own ideas. In the first year they unravel and evaluate critically what those ideas are, and in the second year they are evaluating the law and whose interest is being protected.

(Law tutor)

Students have a problem of not being selective and knowing what is essential information, so in their writing there tends to be too much description rather than the development of a structured argument. Also they often lack an understanding of the link between theory and evidence. They need to be able to evaluate theory using evidence as support and write a structured essay which develops logically. A lot of students have difficulties setting something up, arguing it through and bringing it to a

conclusion. Although a standard 2.2 answer may give accurate information most students are not using argument skills. Writing clearly and well
with clarity is important, and I focus as much on the written style as on
the content but I know that some of my colleagues focus more on the
content. I am looking for the ways in which students use the structure of
their writing to convey their point. Getting underneath the problem is a
difficulty for students. If you don't get a central concept right then how
can you argue about it if you do not know what you are talking about?
Sometimes students don't pick up on the central issues. They learn to put
one theory followed by another one and then end up by saying they don't
know the answer. This is a typical 2.2 answer which is limited in its scope
of the real grasp of the argument. Of course, many mature students are
trying to unlearn and develop new ways of thinking. They have to learn
not to think about what they are doing as an office manager but to think
about it as a psychologist.

(Psychology tutor)

Students are meant to be putting answers into words for a manager but
sometimes they just analyse the last number they come to and that is the
answer. We try to use model answers but the problem with model answers
is that there is not really a model answer. What we are looking for is
various key points in some kind of logical order and the conclusion to
follow from the evidence. Students often lack any appreciation of the real
issue that they are meant to be looking at and do not know how to put
maths into writing and into solving real-life problems. So they look at the
key word and dump everything on the page that they have heard about it
instead of developing a logical argument around the subject. In management sciences students are working across disciplines; they are combining
with languages, psychology, accounting, economics and in essence can
come from any subject area. In some ways students have less difficulty
adapting to writing in management science than they do in adapting to
other subjects because it is more flexible and more common sense; it is less
related to the literature. Students are encouraged to include examples
from their own experience and are less oriented towards textbook theory
than other subjects.

(Management sciences tutor)

Students have difficulties with organization and knowing how to use
primary texts. They often fail to build the essay around the text. They
need to be able to organize an argument, answer the question and learn
to play with the terms of the question. There is a need to be able to find
appropriate quotations, and once students have the quotes they should
use these for analytic purposes or to further an argument. One of the
problems with 'post-structuralist' theories in the humanities is that
writing such theory takes you away from where the students are. Students

exposed to these discourses begin to parrot these discourses. We do need to find ways of introducing students to these discourses without their parrot-phrasing it in their own writing.

(English tutor)

The assessments include problem-solving exercises, writing essays, practicals, answering short questions, mini-tests, theoretical projects and a comprehension exercise. We are testing the students' ability to read and critically evaluate a paper, and their writing and comprehension skills. Students are also asked to write an abstract for talks they are giving. There are no clear guidelines for written work but it has to have some structure and content and be well laid out and argued. In some essays we are looking for factual information and in others looking at things in much broader global terms. By the third year writing is much more about how students are processing the information and not just the facts.

(Biology tutor)

What you should notice as you read through the comments of these tutors is that they are all asking for something slightly different from their students' writing. In other words, there is no one way of academic writing. It is important to keep this point in mind as you approach each new written assignment. As we said, one of the best ways of finding out what is required for any particular piece of written work is to ask your tutor. Since your tutor is most likely to be the person to mark your work, it is useful to establish what their guidelines are about written work. Your tutor will probably have set 'office hours' when they will be able to answer students' queries. Increasingly, tutors are also making their email addresses available to students. The sorts of question you may be asking, depending on the subjects that you are studying, are listed below:

Questions to ask the tutor

- Should I say what exactly I am going to do in my introduction?
- How do I incorporate the quotes I use?
- How do I set out and refer to charts, diagrams and tables?
- What do you mean when you say 'use evidence to support my argument'?
- In my last essay I was told that I needed to 'develop an argument'. Could you explain exactly what that means?
- Is this to be written in the form of a report or an essay, or is it a different kind of writing altogether?
- How do I use theory to describe my practical professional experience?
- I do not really understand the essay question. Could you give me a bit more information about it?
- Can I use 'I' in my essay?
- Is it all right to quote from newspaper articles?

- I know what I want to say but I just cannot get it down on paper. Is there any advice that you could give me for this particular assignment?
- What sorts of thing should I be putting in the conclusion?

3.4 Key elements of university writing

The tutors quoted above all had slightly different ways of describing their students' writing but often used a similar kind of terminology (what we call 'key elements') to describe what they were looking for. Below is a list of some of the more commonly used key elements for university writing. You will often find that feedback on your work may refer to these and you can expect to have to include some of them in the different kinds of written assignment that you will encounter during your studies. Each time you write you will probably be using a number of these key elements in some form or other in your writing. The tutors who mark your work will be looking out for the things that they think are most important, but as you will have seen from the above examples, they will not all be looking for the same things. It is useful for you to find ways of identifying at what points in your writing you are drawing on these elements. The following activity is designed to help you to do that.

Activity Seven: Looking for key elements

Choose an assignment that you are working on at the moment. Work through the following list and consider which key elements are likely to apply to this particular assignment.

Key elements of university essay writing

- Developing an argument
- Linking theory and evidence
- Drawing a conclusion
- Analysing
- Being critical
- Developing a central idea
- Processing information
- Incorporating facts
- Correct terminology
- Logical order
- Use of evidence to support an argument

- Use of primary texts
- Use of quotations
- Drawing on personal experience
- Expressing own opinions
- Using personal interpretation

If you have difficulties deciding which key elements will be relevant, then try completing the activity with a student who is writing the same assignment.

3.5 Different ways of knowing

You have probably begun to get a sense by now of the complexity of academic writing and why it can often seem rather a daunting task when you are faced with your written course assignments. You may be asking yourself the following questions:

- How can I learn to recognize what each writing task is about?
- How can I learn to be a competent writer in all my different courses?

If you look back to Chapter 2, you will see that we emphasized the importance of asking questions at each stage of writing. The following activity develops this idea by getting you to ask questions about a number of your own assignments.

Activity Eight: Comparing two assignment titles

Find two assignment titles that you are working on from different courses at the moment. They may be courses in the same subject areas or 'fields of study' (for example, both broadly history courses), or they may be from different areas altogether (for example, European studies and English).

Take a blank piece of A4 paper. At the top of the page write the two assignment titles that you have chosen.

Now look at the list of questions below. As you work through the list write down your answer in relation to the assignment titles that you have chosen. For this particular exercise it is best to avoid note form. Try to write your answers in complete sentences. Imagine that you were going to ask somebody to read this, so you should make sure that it makes sense to the reader.

- Are the two assignments from the same subject area?
- How do you think they seem similar?

- How do you think they seem different?
- Would you describe the kind of writing that is being asked for as an essay or as something else – for example, a report, a commentary, a summary?
- Will you need to quote from sources in writing this assignment?
- How will you reference other authors in this assignment?
- What sources (books, articles, reports, handouts) will you need to help you to write the assignment?
- Will you use any of the following in preparation: lecture notes; books and articles by recognized authors on the same topic; official reports; primary sources (a poem, a novel, an original historical document); secondary sources (what somebody else has written about the above, for example, a book on literary criticism); graphs, charts and diagrams?

When you look at what you have written you should be able to see just how varied the writing tasks from different courses may be and how approaching them in this way can help you to focus on how to analyse each one. Each time that you are confronted with a new piece of work you can use this kind of analysis to help you work out how you are going to approach your writing at this very early stage. We develop this approach to analysing the assignment in more detail in the next chapter.

The following quote from Lizzy, a first-year undergraduate, might also help you to understand some of the difficulties that so many students experience with the requirements of different courses, particularly in their first year at university.

The trouble is that coming from A levels it all seems so different here. When I did my A levels I never had any difficulties writing essays. In all our courses we were given dictated notes and wrote essays from these notes. We weren't expected to use a number of different sources or make any choices about what we used in our essays. I think that was one of the reasons I came unstuck with my writing when I got to university. I found it really difficult to introduce arguments and use different authors' opinions in history. In fact I had real problems with my first history essay. I'd never done history at school, well not since before GCSE, and I just wrote this essay using one book. That was the way we'd learned in English. I had no idea that you had to read one author and set one idea against another. Although we had lots of advice on essay writing it was all about the technical things, referencing and all that, not about the really difficult bits like structure and argument. The thing is that in Spanish everything here is centred around this one sort of textbook, so again you don't really have to use other ideas much. That makes it easier to write an essay. And of course it's the same in English. You just relate the essay to a particular text. I'm doing drama as well and there we have a list of what's needed, we don't have to write an argument or anything. It's about things like stage plans. The thing I've learnt now about history is that it's all about for or against and criticizing one argument with another. Although I would like to put forward my own point of view I'd never say anything like 'I think'. I'd have to say something like 'it could be argued' or 'general opinion would be'. Sometimes I have used 'I' in the conclusion but it would depend a bit on who my tutor was.

3.6 Structure and argument

If you look back at the quotes from the tutors you will see just how many of them refer to the notion of 'structure' and 'argument'. Lizzy also talks about these concepts. We will be looking at this further and in more detail in Chapters 6 and 7. What we can say at this stage is that argument and structure are not tangible concepts, as one lecturer said:

> I can recognize a good piece of student writing when I see it. I know when it is well structured and has a well-developed argument but it is difficult to say exactly what I am looking for, let alone describe a good argument more fully.

3.7 The traditional essay format approach to writing

If you look back over this chapter you will see that we have made reference to the idea of a traditional essay, although, as we have said, in practice you are likely to come across many different ways of writing during your studies. The more traditional academic essay will have an introduction, which sets the scene; a main body, in which you outline and develop your argument; and a conclusion, in which you bring everything together. Advice about essay writing usually gives instructions as to how to go about and successfully complete this type of writing at university in the way laid out below:

- Introduction: What is this essay going to be about?
- Main body: What are the themes that I am developing to support my argument?
- Conclusion: What are the consequences of what I have written?

In our experience many students find it very easy to identify this kind of format and know that they have to start with an introduction, develop their ideas in the main body and then bring everything to a neat and satisfactory conclusion. In practice, of course, following this kind of format is much more complicated than it seems; many students struggle with getting their ideas down on paper despite knowing in theory what the finished product should look like. Although this framework may be useful as a general rule of thumb for some of your writing, you are likely to find that many of your assignments do not fit neatly into it. You may find it more useful to think of this idea of breaking down the essay into three parts as just one approach to assignment writing. Another approach which we develop below is the 'building blocks' approach, which can give you a general feel for the structure of the assignment that you are writing. The chapters that follow develop the notion that you are creating and building your own structure in your writing as you work through the process of writing a particular assignment. In essence, you are moulding your knowledge – through your writing – to the task, the written assignment.

3.8 The 'building blocks' approach to writing

Writing assignments is about finding the right building blocks each time and putting them together in a coherent order. In the same way that using the same raw materials is unlikely to result in two identical buildings, even if you use the same sources and answer the same question no two assignments will ever be exactly the same. If we look back to the tutors' comments we can see how repeatedly they use words and metaphors linked with building as ways of describing student writing in their own subject areas; if it is difficult to describe something one way, then coming to the same thing from another direction can often help. We can use metaphors in this way to help understand how to develop structure and argument in our academic writing. These are some of the words and phrases tutors and students use to describe writing assignments:

Structuring
Building blocks
Support
Model
Linking
Mixing
Body
Processing
Getting underneath

Centre
Construction
Shaping

Using 'building blocks' is a metaphorical way of thinking about writing, which we hope will be helpful to you when you come to a new assignment. As you approach each new assignment, you, the writer, are the 'apprentice' but your tutor is more likely to be an 'experienced builder'. Although a more experienced academic writer may be able to describe in very general terms what a finished structure – the written assignment – could look like, that does not necessarily help you with the actual process of writing. Your tutor will be able to tell you where you went wrong with your writing after the finished structure is completed. What you have to remember is that at this stage, although you may feel like an 'apprentice' you are actually in charge of the building. As the writer you have to be able to identify the building blocks and put them together in a way that makes sense. In Chapter 2 we discussed brainstorming and illustrated the use of a spider diagram. These are useful techniques to use now to identify the building blocks, the different parts of your assignment. In Chapter 6 we look at the ways in which you can build from topics and themes to support your argument and illustrate this with the use of a mind map. Using these visual representations can be helpful in identifying the building blocks that you may decide to use in your particular piece of writing. Whatever piece of academic writing you are attempting, whatever subject or course you are doing, you will be putting together all the components into a structured coherent whole. You will be the one to have to make choices about the sources you will be drawing from, what to put in and what to leave out, and what are the most important points to make in answering the question. Assignment writing is never about writing down everything that you know about the subject. It is always about addressing a specific question and answering it in such a way that your tutor is able to assess how well you have understood that aspect of the course. In the next chapter we will be examining how you start from the title and begin writing. Before we move on, it will help you to have completed the activities set in this chapter because, in themselves, they are the building blocks of what is to follow.

Notes

- There is no one way of academic writing.
- Courses may ask for a variety of ways of writing, even if they are broadly within the same 'field of study'.
- Be prepared to write – and think – in different ways for different assignments and for different parts of courses.
- Tutors will have their own understandings of what constitutes a good piece of student writing.

- Ask your tutor what he or she is looking for in your written work.
- Find out if it is possible to email your tutor as an alternative to seeing them personally.
- Visual representation (spider diagrams, mind maps) can help you identify your building blocks for writing.
- Writing an assignment is about more than knowing you have three parts to an essay.

4

Beginning with the title

*Keywords • Disadvantages of just looking for keywords • Analysing
the assignment*

I can't answer this. I don't understand the question.

Students often don't answer the question that has been set.

I can't answer this, I don't know anything about it.

We saw in the previous chapter how you are likely to find it necessary to write
in different ways for different courses during your time at university. This
chapter will look at ways of developing strategies to analyse and work with
your assignments, which should help you to approach the different pieces of
writing that you have to do. It builds on the activities that we have suggested
so far. We will begin with the title. One criticism frequently levelled at students
by lecturers is that students do not answer the question. One lecturer put it
like this:

> When my students ask me about essay writing, there are three main pieces
> of advice that I give them. One, answer the question. Two, answer the
> question. Three, answer the question.

At the same time, students often complain that they find it difficult to work
out what the question is asking of them. When they seek advice they may find
that they receive the kind of response that this student experienced:

> I didn't really understand the question, none of us did, so I went to my
> tutor and asked what it meant and how I should write it. She said that she

could not give me any further advice because that was the point of the exercise, to work out how to answer the question.

Despite this student's experience, our advice to you is that initially, if you really are having difficulties answering a particular assignment question, then you should go to your tutor and ask his or her advice. We have made this point previously and we will be making it again throughout the book. However, we hope that by the time you have worked through this chapter you will feel more confident in tackling questions which seem daunting and unfamiliar.

4.1 Keywords

One way that students are often taught to approach a new title is to pick out the keywords and work with these to understand how they should approach the assignment. A student described how she had used this approach at A level:

My strategy for dealing with the essay title is one that I learned at school. Basically, I pick out keywords from the title and plan my structure around that. Then I try to write from this, putting together the introduction, the main body and lastly the conclusion. The trouble is that I keep getting blocked and can't get any further with the writing. When I try to write from the plan then I just drift off when I'm writing.

With the keywords approach you pick out what seem to be the important parts of the question and ignore the linking words. The focus is on leaving out the less important linking words and picking out both the content keywords (what the assignment is about) and the academic keywords such as those in the list below:

Academic keywords

Discuss

Explain

Compare and contrast

Describe

Analyse

Illustrate

Evaluate

Outline

Critically examine

Assess

Activity Nine: Identifying academic keywords

One way of usefully working with the academic keywords of the question is to spend some time thinking about the meanings of these words. Look at the above list. Look over some of the questions for written assignments in your course.

- Do they use any of these words?
- Why do you think the lecturer has used a particular academic keyword rather than another?
- Write down your own ideas about what the academic keywords mean (do not use dictionary definitions).

4.2 Disadvantages of just looking for keywords

Although we feel that looking for the keywords can be a useful starting point, as we hope you will have learnt by trying out Activity Nine, there are two main reasons why we want to help you to go further in your approach to answering the question.

First, the keywords approach 'locks you in' to the academic wording of the question. In our experience, for students successfully to unpack the question that they have either been set or chosen to answer, they need to 'translate' the question into words and language that make most sense and feel most familiar to them. This is part of what we were asking you to do in Activity Nine.

Second, the keywords approach tends to be most useful for traditional 'academic essays' but less useful for other kinds of assignment writing. The traditional academic essay question is often characterized by the use of academic keywords like those listed above. Focusing on these does not help very much if you have to write an assignment which is not in the form of a traditional academic essay. If we really want to understand the complexity of a question, then we need to do more than identify either the academic keywords or the content keywords. What is really important is for you to work on developing your own sense of what a particular assignment title means. You will need to get to grips with and grasp the meaning of the whole question and not just some bits of it. In the next section we illustrate a method that we believe should be able to help you approach any written assignment that you have to complete during your time as a university student.

4.3 Analysing the assignment

The following five points outline a method for analysing your own writing tasks, beginning with the title. Read through these first and then read through the three examples. The three examples illustrate how this method can be used with different types of written assignment in different subject areas.

1. *Write down in your own words what you think the assignment is asking you to do.* The purpose of this exercise is to get you to consider the question in your own words and through your own ways of expressing things, using language that feels comfortable and familiar to you. Try to describe and write down what you think this assignment is asking for in your own terms rather than in 'academic language'. This will help you to make more sense of the question. This is an important part of the analysis. It can take a lot of time to do and you might find it difficult, particularly if you are approaching a question which you do not feel very confident about answering. For this reason we suggest that you do not use notes for this section but write out what you are thinking in full. If you find this difficult to begin with, then use a tape recorder and answer this section from your own tape recording. You could also talk it over with another student. You should be able to see from the examples below how you might be likely to approach your own assignment analysis.

2. *What do you already know about the subject matter of the assignment?* Once you have begun to analyse the question you can start to relate your analysis to what you already know about the subject matter. Answering the question and writing the assignment are never just about putting down everything that you know about a subject. What you know has to be presented in relation to the question that has been set. This is why at this stage it is useful to begin to think about what you know in terms of the assignment title. Write down what you already know and how this relates to the title. If you find it easier you can use notes to complete this section.

3. *What do you need to know to help you complete this assignment successfully?* This might seem a strange question – how can you know what you don't yet know? However, you will find that this question does help you to begin to focus on the gaps in your knowledge. By this stage you have got some way into analysing the title and begun to think about what you know already, and how this knowledge can be used to help you to write your assignment. Starting from your analysis of these things so far, you will be able to identify in general terms what you will need to know more about before you can get going with the writing. You might find it helpful to use a spider diagram at this stage. Then it might be easier to see the gaps, the missing bits that you need to help you complete the writing task that has been set.

4. *How do you think this assignment differs from or is similar to other assignments that you are working on at the moment?*

In Activity Eight we asked you to compare different assignment titles, and working on that task will help you with this section. As we illustrated in Chapter 3, students frequently find that they are having to work on quite different pieces of written work at the same time (see also Chapter 12). We cannot stress enough how important it is to consider each assignment as a piece of writing in its own right. Each assignment title needs its own analysis. Of course, as you become more proficient in writing at university you will become much quicker at unpacking each title and each piece of written work. We feel that one way of helping you to do this is to get you to be able to feel the contrast and differences between the assignments that you are having to complete. This is why this section is concerned with contrast and getting you to identify the similarities and differences between assignments. This is particularly worthwhile if you are taking a modular degree course because what you have to write, and the way in which you write, can be very varied across courses and between different disciplines and subject areas.

5. *How are you going to choose your reading material?*

Choosing what you need to read is an important part of the process of writing an assignment. There is no point in just choosing a book which seems to be related to the subject of the assignment. What you need to do is to consider carefully what you are going to need to complete this particular piece of work and then choose your material accordingly. The reading list that you have for the course is there to help you and should be your starting point. It is not enough just to look at the titles of books, you need to make full use of indexes when you are choosing what to read. The index will help you to decide whether a particular book will be useful for this particular assignment. If you really have trouble getting hold of books from the library then consult your tutor about alternative reading that would be helpful. Additionally, searching the library catalogue can help to throw up other related source material and you can then check the indexes of any likely books for their suitability. In Chapter 8 we examine using sources in more depth, and in Chapter 12 we also explore using the Internet to search for resources to help you with your assignment.

Now, using the numbered headings above we are going to work through three examples of analysing assignments.

Example A

' "A reading of *Kim* tells us more about the British than about India." Discuss.'

1. *Write down in your own words what you think the assignment is asking you to do.*

This essay is asking me to think about the book *Kim* by Rudyard Kipling and the way in which it describes the British in India during the time of colonial rule. Although an obvious way of looking at the book would be to analyse what it tells us about India at that time, this assignment is asking me to do something rather different and to look at the book in a particular way. The word 'discuss' is probably quite important here since the question is framing things in a way which suggests that the book can actually give us more understanding about the British in India than about India and Indian culture. I think that is why the lecturer has used the word 'discuss'. I do not think that he wants me to just put forward the view of the quote in the essay title. I think he wants me to argue against this in some way and to put forward different points of view using examples from the text, the book *Kim*, as evidence, if you like, to support my point of view and what I think in relation to the viewpoint put forward in the essay title. I would use quotes from the text to support my ideas. So I really have to do two things here, I think: on the one hand, find evidence in the text to support the views expressed in the quote; and on the other, put forward some alternative viewpoints, and for this I would need to find examples in the text to help support what I wanted to say. I have not read the book yet so I cannot say a lot more about the question at this stage. But I will be using ideas that I have learnt in other parts of my course to help me to understand and analyse the text.

2. *What do you already know about the subject matter of the assignment?*
   I don't know much about the subject matter because I haven't actually read the book yet. However, this is part of a course on literature about British colonial rule in India and so I do have some background knowledge from the other novels that I have read and also a bit from a biography of Rudyard Kipling that is on our reading list.

3. *What do you need to know to help you complete this assignment successfully?*
   Basically, I really need to know the book well so that I can analyse the text and make sense of the question. I think I also need to do some historical reading about the British in India, which is on our reading list, and I haven't done any of that yet. With this kind of essay I think that the main thing is to know the book really well and use quotes to support what I want to say. I expect I will use my lecture notes as well, which are not particularly about this book but will give me a better idea how to approach the subject matter of the question.

4. *How do you think this assignment differs from or is similar to other assignments that you are working on at the moment?*
   I'm writing another assignment for an early drama course at the moment. That's a bit different and in a lot of ways it is much easier than this one. In the drama course there doesn't seem any need to develop any kind of argument or put forward different points of view. It just seems to be describing a particular play and the stage settings of it, that kind of thing. We have been given some very clear guidelines on how to do this.

5. *How are you going to choose your reading material?*
   Mostly, I shall use the actual novel but we do have a good reading list. If I'm stuck on the background bits about the British in India, then either I will ask my tutor or I'll try to do a library search.

Example B

'Working in pairs, use the following question to put together a written portfolio: Outline the key developments in the women's suffragette movement between the 1860s and the First World War. Why was there opposition to its growth?'

1. *Write down in your own words what you think the assignment is asking you to do.*
   This is really different to anything that I have done before. It's what is called a portfolio for history – we have to collect together different kinds of material, and we have to pair up with someone else so I'm not quite sure exactly how that is going to work out. There are really two parts to it: there's the bit we present in our seminar, which we do together, and then the writing bit that we actually do on our own. Although the title is broken up, so that it seems that there are two separate bits to this assignment, I think I would really tend to put them together in my writing. I wonder what it really means, using the word 'outline'. It sounds as if you just have to list the actual events and things that happened between those dates. Although I haven't really ever done any history before, I know that it is very unlikely that we are just meant to be listing and describing things. Anyway the second part, I think, is probably the key because we have to suggest reasons for people being against the suffragettes. To do that I have to know what else was going on at the time and why people might have been thinking the way that they were. I suppose I have to put together getting the right facts and dates with some kind of analysis of why things might have happened in a particular kind of way and at a particular time. I also need to talk about not just how the suffragette movement developed but why it developed in that way, bearing in mind other things that were going on politically and socially at that time. Of course, it would be the other things that were going on in the economic, political and social climate that would influence the support or opposition that the suffragettes might experience. So although on first reading it looks quite simple, it is actually quite complex. It is not just a question of knowing that the movement developed in a particular way or that people were opposed to it. It's more analysing why the movement developed in that way in the light of other things happening at the same time. It's also about being able to understand and analyse the opposition as people would have seen it at that time.

2. *What do you already know about the subject matter of the assignment?*
   I don't really know much yet about the suffragettes, except about the general bits that we have done in lectures about what was going on at this

time and where the movement developed from. I certainly need to be clearer about the chronology of a lot of different events at that time, what came before or after what. I do know how the analyses of historical events are closely linked to one another, we've done a lot about that in our lectures. I will be using this idea in my portfolio – that is, that the suffragette movement didn't just happen in isolation. I know that a lot of people were opposed to the suffragettes because they were women but I am not really clear about it.

3. *What do you need to know to help you to complete this assignment successfully?*
Because we have to put together a portfolio I need to read some bits of original documents, maybe from writers or newspapers of the time, which I can use as my sources and evidence. I'll need to be able to analyse these to answer the question and particularly to provide evidence of the opposition to the suffragettes. This is quite a bit longer than an essay and we get 60 per cent of our marks on this course for this so it's important that I put a lot of work into it. The other thing is that I need to do quite a bit of reading, not just about the suffragette movement but also about the way that things were changing at the time, things like the beginnings of the Labour Party and the effect this could have had on people's thinking about women's issues. When I am writing this I am going to have to know the different positions of different writers because I cannot just write from one viewpoint. I'll have to put forward different historians' ideas and interpretations of what was going on at the time. We've got a really good reading list with this course, so I'm going to try the library and see what I can get hold of. If that doesn't work, my tutor says that she has copies of some of the most important chapters and articles that we can borrow from her office.

4. *How do you think this assignment differs from or is similar to other assignments that you are working on at the moment?*
Well basically, although it looks like an ordinary essay question, it is much more in depth because we have to present a portfolio. There are two good things about it which make it easier in some ways. One is that we have to work together with someone else, and the other is that we have to make a seminar presentation before we actually get down to the writing of it. This means that I can get some ideas from the other people in my seminar group and from my tutor at the seminar. So I'll try to make notes of the important things that come out of that and put those in my portfolio. Although we actually work in pairs a lot, the final writing of the portfolio is something we do on our own. It's also a bit different because we have to merge together so many different things, using original documents, primary and secondary sources, but still finally presenting a sort of argument once we have put everything together.

5. *How are you going to choose your reading material?*
I've already answered this but I suppose the only bit to add is how I'll choose what to read once I have got hold of the books on the reading list for this

course. I shall be really careful to check the index because once I just went for the chapter that looked as if it was the most relevant. I missed another really important part of the book because I was in a rush, and couldn't be bothered to go and plough through the index and look up all the references for the subject I was writing the essay about. Because of that I missed an important bit in my essay and got a really bad mark for it. It meant that I missed out a whole lot of important ideas because they were not in the chapter I had been looking at. I think it's really important to look at the index carefully and not just look at the titles of the chapters in books.

Example C

'Detail some of the methodological and theoretical problems raised by the collection and representation of linguistic data, with specific reference to your own project.'

1. *Write down in your own words what you think the assignment is asking you to do.*
   This is a really difficult question, but it is a compulsory first assignment for this course. I am not really sure how to go about answering the question because until now we have always had to write our essays using books and articles. In fact, sometimes we've been quite discouraged from bringing in pieces of our own research. I think fundamentally we have to put together two rather different parts of this assignment. The first part is to present in some way the linguistic data that we have collected. We have to transcribe 10 minutes of an interview or conversation. I checked that with the tutor. The second part is about analysing the problems that we had with collecting the data and relating this to the theories that we have read and the things that we discussed in our seminars. These are theories about language, speaking and communication. So I would start with the theories of various authors and then try to fit our bit of research into what these authors say. I suppose another thing could be that our research does not really fit with the theoretical analyses that we have learnt about, so therefore it could make it more difficult to understand and describe.
2. *What do you already know about the subject matter of the assignment?*
   I know about something called the 'ethnography of communication' which is definitely a good starting point for this, but there are a lot of things I really need to read before I decide how to describe the difficulties that I had with the analysis. On our reading list and in the seminars we have talked about the relationship between ways of saying things and using language, and issues of power and authority, but I haven't really read anything about this yet. Before I can talk about the problems of analysing and collecting the data I have to have a framework for my analysis. I think that knowing what certain authors have to say about language and power is crucial in helping me with my analysis.

3. *What do you need to know to help you to complete this assignment successfully?*
   I've really answered this already in the previous section because I am more aware of the things that I haven't read in terms of this question. One of the bits that I really need to understand more fully is what people really mean by 'methodology'. This word is always coming up and I never really know exactly what it means. It's obviously really important now that we are being asked to do our own bit of research. There are some books and articles on our reading list which I think might help with this. The other thing I think I'll do is talk to other people on this course about what they think it means. I feel really stupid asking the tutor.

4. *How do you think this assignment differs from or is similar to other assignments that you are working on at the moment?*
   This is really completely different to anything that I have had to do before. Firstly, we do the tape recording and collect the data in teams, then we have to transcribe the material, and then we have to write this assignment. The writing is obviously entirely our own piece of work. We've already decided that we are going to record some children in the university crèche at what they call 'show and tell' time. When we write it up it will be very different to presenting an argument in the way that I'm used to. Normally I sort of write what different authors have said and then sort of link them together and balance them all up with my own ideas. That's really how I put together an argument. In this case the whole point seems to be to relate what the theories on analysing language and communication have to say about my own data. Our tutor has asked us to attach the transcript to the back. So in the writing I'll have to be referring to this and to what other authors say which seems relevant. At the moment I can't quite see how that kind of writing will work out because I don't want it just to be a series of long quotes from the transcripts. The other thing that I'm not really sure of is whether it is going to be all right to say 'I' or 'we' or 'the researcher'. I'll probably risk 'I' and hope that is OK.

5. *How are you going to choose your reading material?*
   Basically, I'm just sticking to the reading list because it is quite compre-hensive and will give me what I need to help me to analyse our data.

The three examples above illustrate how students use their own understand-ings of an assignment title to guide their thinking on writing and their choice of reading. None of these individual examples will be exactly right for you and your writing, but they should be able to give you ideas about a general approach to analysing written assignments. This kind of analysis does not go into detail about all the content of your essay, but it can help you to see:

- what you think the question is asking you to do;
- what you already know;
- what you might need to develop further;
- what gaps you have in your knowledge and what you need to find out.

Don't forget the examples are from students who are looking at the assignment title for the first time. In a sense they are first thoughts on a written assignment, but they are also the beginnings of focusing and getting ready for writing. We have already seen how lecturers say that students do not read the question; they also say that students seem to think that it is enough just to put in everything that they know about the topic without attending to the actual title. You will see from our examples that the students above all knew something about the topic that they were writing about; as they set about analysing the title they realized not only what they knew but also what they didn't know. They were considering their knowledge specifically in relation to the assignment title. The activity below is designed to help you to apply this approach to one of your own assignments.

Activity Ten: Analysing your own assignment title

Choose a written assignment that you are about to start working on and write the title at the top of a blank piece of A4 paper. Work through the five points above. Use the examples as a guide if you need to. Remember that ultimately it is your analysis and understanding of the title that counts when you come to write.

1. Write down in your own words what you think the assignment is asking you to do.
2. What do you already know about the subject matter of the assignment?
3. What do you need to know to help you to complete this assignment?
4. How do you think this assignment differs from or is similar to other assignments that you are working on at the moment?
5. How are you going to choose your reading material?

From the analysis you have done it can be helpful to make a spider diagram, maybe one for each section. Then this can give you an overall plan and you can see what bits are missing and how you need to fill these gaps before you can reasonably start writing.

At the end of this activity you should have learnt how to unpack the title and work on any kind of written assignment that you come across during your studies. Although we have called this activity 'Analysing your own assignment title' it is a technique that can usefully be used at any time throughout the writing process. It is a good idea, as a check, after you have done your reading and before you start writing, to go through this exercise quickly again. Use the activity as you write to help you to focus your ideas and to make sure that you are answering the question that you have actually been set rather than the one you would like to answer! You can use these points to keep you focused on the title that you are addressing, and also to help you see where and how you may need to adapt your writing while you are writing. As you become a more experienced academic writer, you will find that it takes you less and less time to go through this process and you will fairly quickly be able to work out what you are doing with each piece of writing.

Notes

- Give yourself plenty of time to analyse the assignment at the beginning.
- Remember to keep the question in mind at all stages of writing the assignment.
- Every assignment needs its own analysis.
- Remember there is unlikely to be one right answer to a question.
- Never answer a question by writing down everything that you know about the topic.
- Putting your analysis on the computer can help you to clarify your thinking at this stage and produce a rough plan before you start writing.

5

Reading as part of writing

*Approaching reading • Choosing your reading for an assignment •
Working with your reading • Thinking about the different texts • Reading
and note taking • Making mind maps from reading • Keeping records •
Making meaning through reading • Reading your own and other
students' work*

I've done some reading but it doesn't seem to be very related to this assignment.

*I take copious notes from all these books and then don't really know what to do
with them for my essay.*

Students don't seem to use the reading lists they are given.

In the previous chapter we saw how choosing your reading material was one
important aspect in analysing the title of your written assignment. Reading
is an integral part of the whole writing process, and therefore this chapter is
concerned with helping you to discover new ways of tackling the reading that
you have to do for your studies. Many, if not most, students find reading
difficult when they first begin to study at university. This is partly because the
material can seem rather unfamiliar, both in terms of the terminology that is
used and because of the ways in which ideas and concepts are written. This can
make reading academic texts seem very different from the kinds of reading
that students are used to. If you are more used to novels, newspapers or reports
then, if you want to be able to make the best use of what you read, you will
need to learn new strategies for university.

One of the techniques of writing successfully in an academic environment is to be able to integrate the important points of what you have read into your own writing. To do this it is necessary to have a clear picture of what you have read, and this in itself entails active and focused reading. The tasks in this chapter will help you to work on making the best use of your reading, through examining different ways that you – the reader – can approach written texts. This is an important point to remember. Just as we have described and talked about different ways of writing, so we also want to introduce you to different ways of reading. The way that you read a text depends on your previous experiences of reading and the way that you adapt these to the new kinds of reading that you will be doing as a student. This is why one of the first activities in this chapter is designed to help you to think about varieties of reading and how you may find these similar or different. Academic reading is often hard work and we hope that as you work through the activities you will find ways which help you to unpack the text and make the most use of what you read in your assignments. We cannot emphasize enough just how important reading is if you are going to write successful assignments. There are few short cuts, but there are ways of making it more manageable and using your time more effectively. Reading is always an integral part of student writing; therefore we think that it is worth spending some time developing strategies which will help you to make the best use of your reading.

Although this chapter is primarily designed to help with the books and articles that you will need to read as part of your studies, in order to write more effectively there is another important way of thinking about reading that we want you to consider. As an effective writer, you are also a reader not only of other authors' work but also of your own. Any of the techniques that you learn in order to approach published, written texts can also be used to edit and work on your own writing. This will enable you to make sure that what you write will make sense to the person who is reading it, your tutor. We will return to this in Chapter 10.

5.1 Approaching reading

With academic reading it is necessary to maintain a constant grip on what the author is saying. Yet, many academic texts are densely written in unfamiliar ways which make them much more difficult to manage than, for example, a novel or a magazine article. Although sometimes there may be reasons why you need to skim-read an article or book, this is likely to be only to get the general gist of what is being said, as a strategy for deciding whether it is appropriate reading material or not. In general, skim-reading is not a useful strategy for reading as a student, but you may well be used to doing this in other contexts, for example, skimming through a newspaper article, or skipping through a novel, not bothering much about learning or pronouncing the names of characters or places, and paying little attention to some of the more complicated parts of the plot. You may also be used to skim-reading when you're surfing the Internet. So now, instead of skim-reading you will be developing ways of concentrating on large chunks of quite dense text and making sense of them. Even though you may only be concentrating for short bursts of time, it is likely that you will find it necessary to concentrate more intensely than you usually do when you are reading. This is why creating the right environment is an important part of approaching your reading. No student can make much sense of their reading unless they can create conditions where they can concentrate effectively on the task in hand. You will need to find the reading environment that suits you best. The list below gives you a few ideas about what may be important, but you will probably want to add to it or modify it to decide what would be best for you.

Creating the right reading environment

- Try to set aside reading time when you will not be interrupted.
- Try to find a physical environment that is conducive to reading: perhaps at home or maybe in the university library.
- Make sure, before you start reading, that you have all the things you might want to use for taking notes and highlighting: A4 paper; index cards; different coloured pens; highlighters; sticky notes; perhaps a laptop computer.
- Make sure that you are comfortable and can write notes from your reading without feeling cramped.
- Take frequent short breaks and during this time try to digest what you have read.
- Don't expect to be able to make any useful sense of your reading if you are tired, stressed or constantly interrupted.
- If you have family commitments you may have to readjust your time priorities and think through how you will fit in your reading time.

5.2 Choosing your reading for an assignment

The initial stumbling block that most students face is choosing their reading. You will remember that this was one element of analysing the assignment. The first thing to do is to consult the reading list for books and articles that seem relevant to your particular assignment. Doing a library search, by keywords or subject, is also useful if the references on your reading list are already on loan from the library. Your tutor should also be able to advise you as to which are the most relevant publications or websites (see Chapter 8). Once you have got a few references you need to be able to decide which will be the most useful to you. At this stage it is important that you pay particular attention to the signposting in the book; this will tell you how the book deals with the subject matter that is relevant to your assignment. Starting with the index, look up relevant words and subject areas until you find the parts of the book that seem most important. Turn to these sections and chapters. Using the section headings as signposts, skip through and see if it looks as if the book deals with the subject matter in a way that will be relevant for your assignment. Do not choose the book if it doesn't seem to be appropriate to your assignment. You may find that you choose a publication that is not as relevant as you first thought. If this happens then leave it to one side and find something relevant for you. There is no point trying to adapt reading material to an assignment when it is not suitable for answering the question. This is a common trap that students fall into. Obviously, it is not always easy to get the general idea of a book by skimming through the headings in a chapter, but spending a little bit of extra time working with the index and checking different sections of the book, before you actually start reading, will ensure that you do not waste as much time reading inappropriate material or trying to adapt what you have read to your needs. As one student put it:

> I knew it wasn't really the right book but I couldn't get hold of anything else because I'd left it a bit late and all the copies of the book that I really needed had gone by the time I got to the library.

Getting hold of publications
Use your reading list.
Ask your tutor.
Note down other up-to-date references that tutors mention in lectures.
Ask other students on your course (remember to work together as much as possible).
Use library search (subject or keyword), online databases, online journals.

Checking a publication for relevance
Check the title.
Check the index.
Turn to relevant chapter.
Check headings.
Check introduction.
Read a short section to get the feel of its usefulness for you.
Check conclusion.
Does it seem relevant to the assignment question?

Photocopying
Use highlighters and different coloured pens to mark your own copy.
Make your notes and annotations on the copy.

Getting hold of books is nearly always a problem for students. Tell your tutors if it is quite impossible to get hold of what you need. They may be able to arrange for a publication that is in heavy demand to be put in a special restricted loan section of the library. Work with other students on your course so that nobody keeps the books for too long. It may be possible to photocopy from books or journals but it is important to check with the library staff about legal restrictions on photocopying.

Although you will benefit from highlighting relevant sections and annotating your own photocopies or even your own books, please do not write on or mark a library book. This is unfair to other students and lecturers because it is quite likely that your reading will not be the same, and what you think are the salient points are unlikely to be theirs. If a book is marked and annotated, in any way, it changes the nature of the book permanently and makes it very difficult for anyone else to read.

5.3 Working with your reading

There seem to be two major difficulties that students have when they are reading academic books and materials. One is struggling with the ways in which things are written. The other is the length of time that things can take to read. Many students express surprise at the need to make repeated readings of the same material. We cannot stress enough that you are likely to find yourself having to read things more than once, and this is in no way to be seen as strange or unusual. Academics themselves find it necessary to 'repeat-read' articles and books. This is in part due to the dense nature of such texts and the fact that so many ideas are packed into the text. To put it another way, ideas are embedded in the text and it can take a lot of rereading to unravel them so that they appear clear and understandable. The first activity in this chapter is designed to help you to see the differences between types of text and identify what you might find particularly hard work about an academic text that you have to read.

Activity Eleven: Thinking about reading

Think about what kinds of things you normally read (novels, reports, newspapers, magazines). First, choose a type of reading that is most familiar to you. Second, choose a book or article that you are having to read at the moment for your studies. You are going to think about the contrast between these two pieces of text.

> Take a blank piece of A4 paper and divide it in half. On one side of the paper put the title of the familiar kind of reading, for example a novel; on the other side of the paper put the title of the academic text.
>
> Now make a list of some of the ways in which you think the two texts appear to be different from one another.

Our list, below, came from comparing a book called *Wild Swans* by Jung Chang (1993), which is an account of her family's history in China, with a book about literacy used on a social anthropology course (Street 1995).

Wild Swans	Social Literacies
Chapter just starts	Use of headings
Generally shorter sentences	Long sentences, e.g. 42 words
Four or more paragraphs to a page	Paragraph may be more than two-thirds of a page in length
I know most of these words	Use of specialist terminology
Easy to understand	Difficult to grasp the main point of what is being said
Use of paragraphs and punctuation (speech marks) to mark new section	Headings to mark new sections
No need for references and footnotes	Use of references and footnotes
Uniform typeface	Use of different typefaces (bold, italics, font size) for different parts of the text
No obvious introduction and conclusion	Introduction at the beginning of each section
Vivid description	Analytical writing
Simple and obvious chain of events	Many different ideas packed into each section
Focus on people, places and events	Focus on concepts and ideas

Below are extracts from the two books to give you a flavour of the difference. The list above elaborates some other comparative features of the two texts which cannot be seen in these two short extracts.

> We are interested in exploring the ways in which, both at home and at school, dominant conceptions of literacy are constructed and reproduced in such ways as to marginalize alternatives and, we would suggest, to control key aspects of language and thought. We hypothesize that the mechanism through which meanings and uses of 'literacy' take on this role is the 'pedagogization' of literacy. By this we mean that literacy has become associated with educational notions of Teaching and Learning

and with what teachers and pupils do in schools, at the expense of the many other uses and meanings of literacy evident from the comparative ethnographic literature.

(Street 1995: 106)

My mother set off to see Comrade Wang one morning on a mild autumn day, the best time of the year in Jinzou. The summer heat had gone and the air had begun to grow cooler, but it was still warm enough to wear summer clothes. The wind and dust which plague the town for much of the year were deliciously absent.

She was wearing a traditional loose pale blue gown and a white silk scarf. Her hair had just been cut short in keeping with the revolutionary fashion. As she walked into the courtyard of the new provincial government headquarters she saw a man standing under a tree with his back to her, brushing his teeth at the edge of the flowerbed.

(Chang 1993: 154)

5.4 Thinking about the different texts

Of course the texts that you have chosen to look at will have different features and your list will not be the same, although there are likely to be some similarities with our example. However, whatever the kinds of text chosen, thinking about the differences that you have identified can help with your reading. If you can see why you find reading a particular article, chapter or book difficult – in other words, what it is about the text and your reading of it that makes it hard – then you are halfway to solving the problem. Think again about why a particular piece of reading seems difficult. Is it because the sentences are very long? Is it because there are a lot of new and unfamiliar ideas being explained? Is it because the vocabulary is new to you? Is it a combination of all three, or is there something else that makes it difficult for you? For example, you may disagree with the ideas expressed in the text and therefore become irritated or bored when reading it. If this happens try to use the text constructively. Examine what it is that you do not like about the text. Think about why you disagree with the author. Sometimes you will find yourself having to read a text that you just do not get on with because it is essential reading. The section below on 'fitting together' reading (see 5.8) should help you tackle a piece of reading despite your initial responses to it.

5.5 Reading and note taking

One way of approaching a new piece of reading is to break it down into manageable chunks and try to assimilate things bit by bit. There is a close correlation here between your reading and your note taking, and this feeds directly into your writing; therefore at this point we are going to deal with these two things together.

> The trouble is that I read what I have to read and then end up with these copious notes and don't know how to incorporate them into my essay.

This is a familiar cry from students. One of the reasons why so many students feel this way is that they do not really know 'why' or more importantly 'how' they are reading and therefore their notes reflect this. In the next activity you will begin to tackle this problem.

Activity Twelve: Global reading

Choose something that you need to read for your studies or for completing an assignment. If the text has headings then use these to guide you with your understanding.

Read what feels to you a manageable chunk of text. This may be a headed section, a chapter or a complete article. Do not try to read more than you can easily manage at any one time. There is no point just going on and on reading, hoping that somehow the content will sink in. When reading an academic text you will often find that you need to read a manageable section before taking stock of where you are. What seems manageable will depend on your own reading style and the kind of text that you are reading. In one case it may be as much as 20 pages, in another situation it may be as little as one or two. Only you, as the reader, can decide what is a manageable chunk.

When you have completed your chosen section write down in one sentence and in your own words what the reading was about. Try to do this without referring back to the text, if possible. Then move on to the next section.

By the time you have finished your reading you should have a number of very general summary sentences which should be able to give you an overall picture of what your reading is about. Be warned, this is not easy to do. It is often very hard indeed to tease out the key ideas from academic writing but this exercise is a starting point for any new piece of reading. It is what we call a 'global reading strategy' and it should point you in the right direction for making initial notes. Once you have mastered this global strategy you will need to begin to read with a more specific and focused strategy and your note taking will reflect this.

Activity Thirteen: Focused note taking from reading

Take a clean sheet of A4 paper. Divide the page into one-third on the left-hand side and two-thirds on the right-hand side. Or do the same with a page on your computer.

On the wider right-hand side take notes as you read which are relevant to your assignment. You may find it useful to use the same categories or headings as the author, or you may find it more useful to make notes under your own headings. Try to summarize in your own words rather than writing down large chunks of the text. Getting things into your own words is about getting ideas into your own ways of thinking about them. This is the first step to owning the ideas that you are going to write about in your assignment.

When you have finished your initial note taking you are going to use the left-hand side of the page. Go through your notes again and make notes of the key points on the left-hand side. Try to do this without referring back to the original book or article. You may want to summarize using headings, or using a spider diagram rather than writing in a traditional format. At this stage it can be useful to use different coloured pens to group similar themes; a highlighter can also be useful.

Having finished this stage you should have what you can genuinely call your notes. You have started with the academic text and made notes on that. Then you have made notes on your notes. These notes are not only in your own words – rather than direct quotes from the text – but also by now probably grouped into different themes and headings from those used in the text that you are reading. Notes made in your own words using different coloured pens (or different font, size and colour), with your own headings and form of organization, will be the most useful to you when you come to write your assignment. Figure 5.1 illustrates one student's example of focused note taking.

5.6 Making mind maps from reading

Some people find that making linear notes from reading does not always work very well for them and they prefer to create a mind map as a more visual representation. This helps them remember what they have read because they can visualize the different notes that they have made and the ways that they

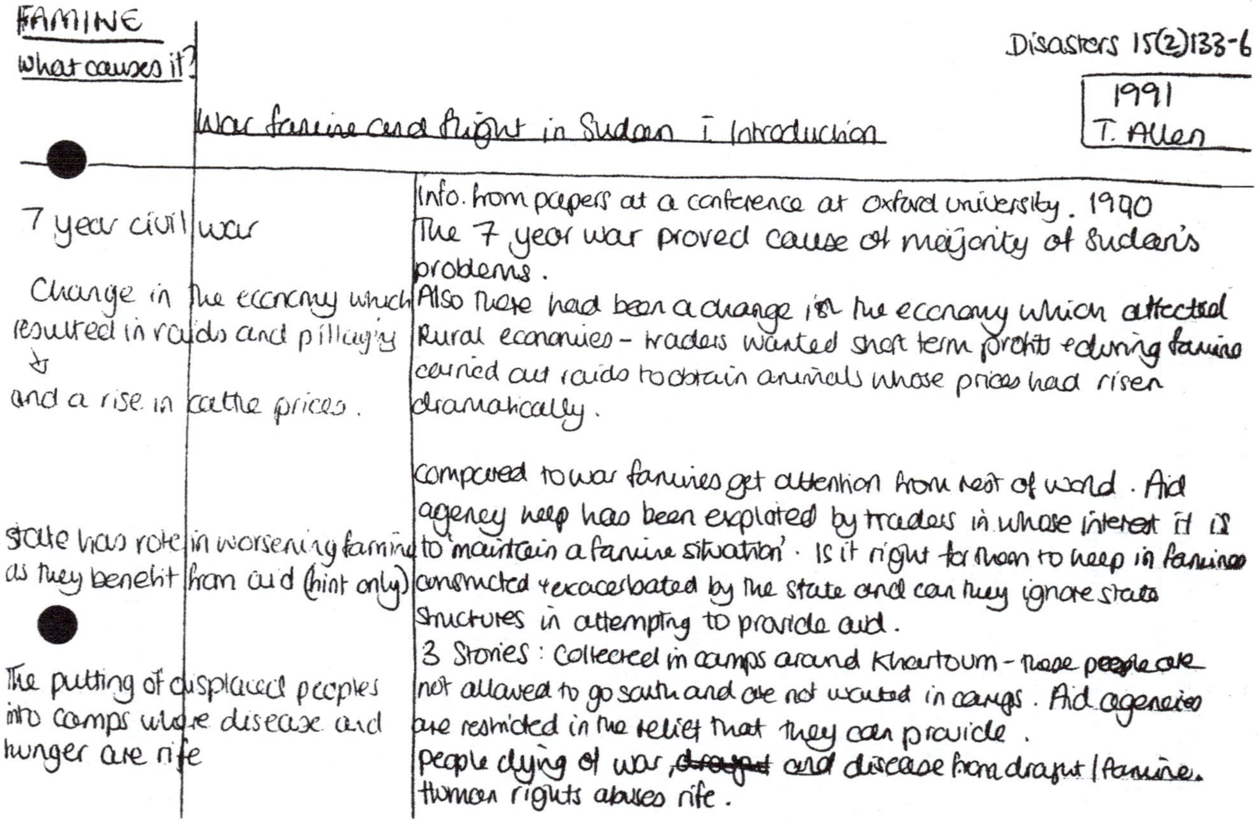

FAMINE
what causes it?

War, famine and flight in Sudan	Introduction

Disasters 15(2)133-6

1991

T. Allen

● Info. from papers at a conference at Oxford university. 1990
The 7 year war proved cause of majority of Sudan's problems.

7 year civil war

Change in the economy which
resulted in raids and pillaging
and a rise in cattle prices.

Also there had been a change in the economy which affected rural economies - traders wanted short term profits reduring farming carried out raids to obtain animals whose prices had risen dramatically.

Compared to war famines get attention from rest of world. Aid

State has role in worsening famine
as they benefit from aid (hint only)

agency help has been exploited by traders in whose interest it is to maintain a famine situation. Is it right for them to keep in famine consenting reconsolidated by the state and can they ignore state structures in attempting to provide aid.

3 Stories: Collected in camps around Khartoum - have people are

The putting of displaced peoples
into camps where disease and
hunger are rife

not allowed to go south and are not wanted in camps. Aid agencies are restricted in the relief that they can provide.

People dying of war and disease hondrought/famine.
human rights abuses rife.

Figure 5.1 Note taking

relate to one another. Below, one student describes how she uses mind maps, not just for reading. Figure 5.2 is an example of one that she did after reading about an area called 'critical discourse analysis' which is concerned with ways of interpreting texts.

I learnt the 'mind map' technique when I was 17, on a weekend course at a women's education centre. A friend who was very arty and picture-thinking said it had changed her life, so I thought I'd give it a go. I took to it really easily. I love the way I can use colours and pictures and my own personal codes. (A little drawing of a sock is often my shorthand for 'socialist'. Word association!) I use mind maps for taking notes in lectures, although I sometimes give up if the lecture is badly structured and I can't tell where it's 'going'. Mind maps need a clear frame but, on the other hand, doing a mind map often generates one. I use them for brainstorming and for essay plans. I tend to take linear notes from books and articles and then synthesize the ideas in a mind map for my essay plan. I give presentations from mind maps and sometimes hand them out, which people like. They're more visually exciting than linear notes. I revise using mind maps. It's so enjoyable to create them; I like to be able to see all the links and everything relevant on one page. I use mind maps to remember or decide what I've got to do that day. I use them for letters and for keeping a journal from time to time. I use them in workshops or for minuting meetings or generating ideas or making decisions. But I still love to write linearly and to craft beautiful prose – but mind mapping helps that process too.

5.7 Keeping records

One good way of recording your references as you go along is to use record cards. On these you can put the referencing information that you need about a book or article that you have read. You can also record brief notes on why you found it useful, you can refer to important page numbers and even record complete quotes if they seem relevant to you. Figure 5.3 shows an example of one such record card, compiled by a student. When she came to write she had much of the information she needed on this author to supplement her other notes. It was also useful when she revisited the same material to write an extended essay later in her course. Of course, you can also use your computer to build up a database of references.

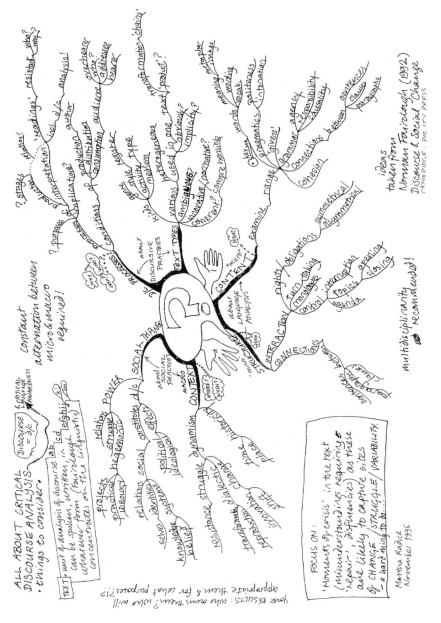

Figure 5.2 Mind map

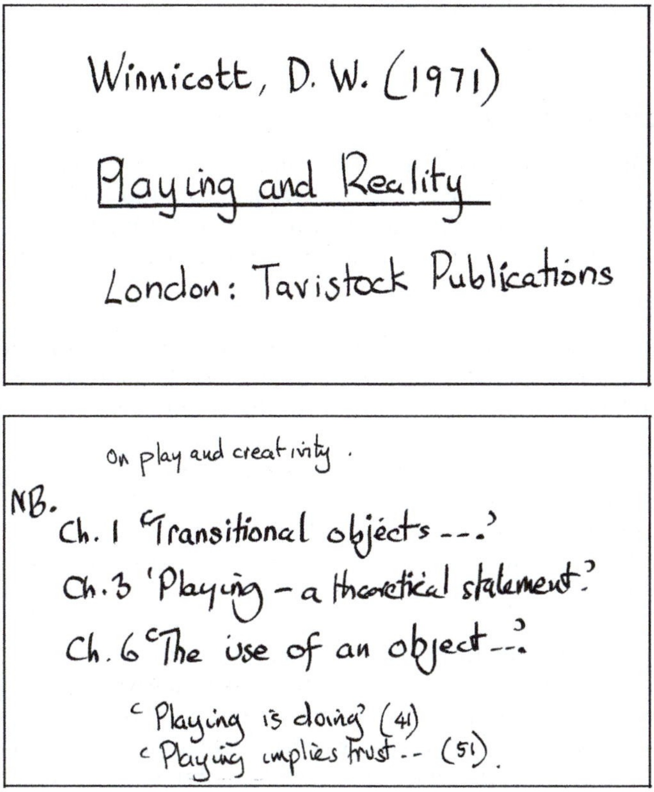

Winnicott, D. W. (1971)

<u>Playing and Reality</u>

London: Tavistock Publications

On play and creativity.

NB.
Ch. 1 'Transitional objects ---.'
Ch. 3 'Playing – a theoretical statement.'
Ch. 6 'The use of an object ---.'

'Playing is doing' (41)
'Playing implies trust --' (51).

Figure 5.3 Reference card

5.8 Making meaning through reading

It is you, the reader, who makes sense of what you read and the meaning that you will be able to make depends to some extent on *how* you are reading. We have already illustrated a method of 'global reading', and below we look at two more ways of 'making meaning through reading' and how you may use these when preparing for your assignments. There are likely to be different reasons for the reading you do for your studies at university. You may be reading as background to your course and seminars, to supplement and elaborate on what you have been taught. You may be reading around a subject that you are thinking of writing about but you feel that you need more information before you can decide if you will be confident in writing an assignment in this area. More commonly, you will be reading to complete a particular assignment.

We are concerned with the latter kind of reading in the two tasks that follow (although we hope that these strategies will be useful to you whatever the purpose of your reading).

'Fitting together' reading

Approaching your reading so that everything that you are reading and studying fits together helps you to focus on your ideas, and both to synthesize and elaborate them. To help you with what we call 'fitting together' reading, try to answer the following questions as you both read and take notes for your reading:

- How does this material relate to what I already know about the subject?
- How does this material relate to other sources on the same subject?
- What related arguments or theories does this reading make me think of?
- How could I use what I am reading in my assignment?
- How could I use this in conjunction with the ideas that I already have on this subject?
- What do I need to add to use this reading constructively in my assignment?
- What do I need to leave out to use this material constructively in my assignment?

You may find it useful to look back to Chapter 4, to the section on 'Analysing the assignment', to see how you might set about answering some of these questions. In fact, analysing the assignment title and 'fitting together' reading are interrelated ways of approaching written assignments. As you read and take notes for your assignment you are working through your analysis of the title and taking from your reading the most appropriate material for your own work.

'Analytic' reading

This is less concerned with reading to fit together with what you know already than with analysing what you are reading as you go along. Again, this is an integral part of the strategy that you will need to adopt to read successfully for your writing. To make the most of analytic reading, these are the sorts of question that you will need to be asking:

- How does the author introduce the text?
- Does she spell out what she is going to talk about?
- What do you think that this author is saying?
- Is the author assuming that you have a particular background knowledge?
- Can you pick out the central thesis or idea of the chapter, book or article?
- Can you understand the different parts of the text and how they all fit together?

- What sort of evidence does the author use to support her argument?
- Does her argument seem biased or one-sided in any way?
- Does her argument seem logical?
- Can you pick out the themes that she uses to support her argument?
- Does her conclusion follow from what she has said or are there some new ideas here?

Activity Fourteen: Trying out different reading strategies

Choose something that you need to read for one of your assignments. Work through the questions above for 'fitting together' reading and 'analytic' reading. Can you identify which kind of reading seems most useful for you at this stage of writing your assignment? You might find that they are equally important.

As we said before, the important thing to remember about reading is that you, the reader, are active in making meaning from what you read. Making sense of what you read is your responsibility, but unfortunately you will find that some academic books and articles are written in ways that make it very difficult for the reader to unpack what the author is trying to convey. We have been emphasizing that the understanding that you get from the text depends to some extent on your own ways of reading. The approaches that we illustrate above are not necessarily kept separate when you are reading. You may well be adopting both at the same time, in a sense reading at a number of different levels simultaneously. You may be reading for very specific information about a topic or subject matter. In that case, you may need to pay particular attention to factual information – for example, dates, names or places. On the other hand, you may be reading to understand much more generally a particular theoretical position – for example, what one psychologist says about child development, as opposed to what another author says about the same thing. In this case, as you read, you will be both analysing the ideas of the author you are reading and comparing them with what you already know. You may be reading a novel or a poem and will therefore be concerned most with interpreting it from your own understanding and perspective.

However you are reading, try to pay attention to the ways in which the author has put the text together:

- If he uses quotes, why has he used them and how has he integrated them into the text?
- If graphs or tables are used how do they fit together? How are these referred to in the text so that the reader knows when to look at them?
- How do different authors reference other sources or use footnotes?

You can use this knowledge when you come to do your own writing. One of the most difficult things about academic writing is incorporating all the different bits and pieces of what you want to say. As we have said, if you pay attention to the work of the authors that you are reading, you will begin to get a flavour of how to do the same things in your own writing.

Pay particular attention to how quotes are used. In student writing it is easy for quotes to stick out like a sore thumb. They need to fit in with the general flow of the text, but how they are used can depend very much on the subject area in which you are writing. It is best to use a quote to support (with references) what you have said or are intending to say. It is unwise to let the quote do the work for you. A quote is always somebody else's words and it is more interesting for the reader to read what *you* have to say rather than a series of quotes interspersed by your words. Thinking about this while you are reading for your studies will help you to get an idea of how to use quotes or cite evidence for yourself. We discuss this in more detail in Chapter 8.

5.9 Reading your own and other students' work

Now that we have worked through these different approaches to reading we want to remind you of what we said right at the beginning of the chapter, that you are also developing these reading strategies as a way of reading and editing your own work. We return to this idea in Chapter 10.

Activity Fifteen: Reading your own and other students' work

Below is an extract from a student essay. Read the essay, and then think about it in relation to the questions that we used for 'analytic reading'.

How do children's semantic mistakes throw light on the process of language acquisition?

Theories of child language acquisition try to explain what processes are taking place as the child develops and uses language effectively. They examine the ways in which the child's linguistic ability is linked to her conceptualizations and perceptions of the world around her. As the child develops her language ability, her language becomes closer to that of the adults in her world and it appears that she attaches the same meanings as the adults around her to the words that she uses. Children appear to pass through remarkably similar stages of language acquisition and make many of the same mistakes. Evidence from research into these mistakes made during the first years of life has enabled some understanding of how language may be acquired. Do children have a conceptual understanding before they develop the ability to refer to an object, situation or state linguistically? Alternatively, does the linguistic identification enable the conceptualization of a particular state? How does a child eventually arrive at the same semantic understanding as most adults for most categories, after what often seems a fairly complex process of trial and error? Why are children so unresponsive to correction in language acquisition? Research has tried to find answers to these questions and has enabled the construction of theories which account for children's development in the use of language, regardless of language or culture.

Researchers have looked, primarily, at three main areas as evidence for the way in which language is acquired:

1. Overextensions
2. Underextensions
3. Overlaps

In these three areas children's language use has been compared with that of adults. Overextensions are very common in children's language, where a child will overextend the use of a word to give it a wider meaning than that normally understood by adults, e.g. 'dog' used for other mammals. Evidence of overextensions in early language development plays a large part in the construction of acquisition theory. Underextensions are more difficult to detect, as they can be easily confused with the child's correct use. A child using 'kitty' for a specific animal and not other cats could be underextending. Overlap, also more difficult to identify, occurs when children use a lexical item with a meaning that overlaps with the adult meaning but where the meaning appears limited, for example, a child using 'car' for all toy cars but not as a general word for car.

Four main theoretical perspectives can be identified as being useful but partial theories of child language acquisition. These are: semantic feature hypothesis; prototype theory; functional core concept theory; and lexical contrast theory. All four perspectives rely on empirical research of children's lexical and semantic errors and attempt to identify the processes through which children attach meaning to lexical representation.

(The student then goes on and describes these four theories and compares and contrasts them with each other, concentrating on the strengths and weaknesses of each position and citing a number of authors who have developed and argued for each particular theory. She concludes her essay as follows.)

From an examination of recent theories of language acquisition it appears that most developments have been a result of identifying those areas of production where children appear to make mistakes. The relationship between the child's overall cognitive development, perceptual understanding and semantic development seems to underlie all attempts to explain what processes are at work as children acquire language. Some theories make reference to the importance of children's non-linguistic abilities, but it seems questionable if it is possible to draw any useful linguistic inferences from these. Such abilities may be non-linguistic in a productive sense but is there any truly non-linguistic comprehension, since children generally live within a world in which they are continually exposed to language? The perceptual categories identified by researchers as non-linguistic can only be identified through linguistic categories. All the theories discussed have thrown some light on language acquisition but none are capable of giving more than a partial explanation for the process that takes place. It is evident that children continue to make mistakes, which indicates a lack of some semantic understanding long after the initial stages of acquisition. Although language is primarily a communicative tool and the child appears to work gradually towards a consensus with adult meanings, it has been shown that children are not open to correction in language learning. This would suggest that they are building up their own understandings of the semantic categories and syntactic structures available to them but are unable to be self-correcting until they reach particular levels of understanding regarding how different categories are related to and interact with one another. General cognitive development enables higher levels of perceptual under-standing to be reached as the child's general interaction with the world around her becomes more complex. At the point where she appears to be understanding more about both syntactic and semantic complexity, the child continues to make mistakes much as an adult searching his mental lexicon for a suitable word in a hitherto unknown situation. The development of the child's language enables a further understanding of the world in which she lives and thus, in turn, the ability for her to use the language available to her and her semantic understanding to structure her world.

This is only a short extract from an essay in a traditional format, but we are using it as an example to show you how you can use the 'analytic' reading strategies to read and work on your own and other peer student writing. This is a good exercise for working with other students on 'analytic' reading. Reading each other's work is a good way both to practise this kind of reading and to help focus on your own writing. If, for example, it is difficult to make the links between the themes or bring out a central idea, then a bit of redrafting would be useful before handing in the assignment. These ideas are taken up again in Chapter 10.

Below are the sorts of comment that a fellow student might make on reading the extract in Activity Fifteen using the 'analytic' reading questions (since this is only an extract we cannot fully address all the questions):

You introduce the essay well by telling me that this is going to be about the ways in which children develop language. Then you go on to make connections with the mistakes that children make and ask some questions about these mistakes and how they eventually stop making them. So I think that I am clear at this stage what the essay is going to be about. On the next bit I'm not really quite clear what you are saying. You identify these three different categories and say that they are evidence about how 'language is acquired', but then you go on to talk about how they are actually about children using language in the wrong way. So, I'm a bit lost here. I think that you are definitely assuming that I have quite a bit of particular background knowledge because you use all sorts of words and concepts, like those four theoretical perspectives, which would be really difficult for somebody who wasn't doing linguistics. But you'd assume that the tutor would know what they were about and she is the one marking it. You use these four theories as evidence for what you want to say and then seem in a sense to really develop your position on the argument in the concluding bit. I think quite a lot of students do that. They outline what other authors say and then at the very end introduce their own interpretation of the evidence. You seem to be challenging the idea of there being 'non-linguistic' categories. The other part of your argument seems to be that all the different theories that you have discussed only give a partial answer to how children acquire language. Your evidence for this is that children go on making mistakes long after they have gone through the initial stages of language acquisition. I think the ideas that you conclude with do relate back to the main body of the essay [not shown] because you have explained what you saw as the limitations of each theoretical position as you went along. You do introduce a new idea here in the conclusion. You talk about the ways in which children are building up both their own ideas of the world and the language to describe it at the same time. Then you say that they cannot really correct their mistakes until they have the level of understanding of how different things are connected and relate to one another. You didn't talk about any of this in the main part of the essay. I suppose in a sense you are using this new idea to support your position that present theories are only partial. In a way you put almost all your argument in the concluding paragraph.

Using this last exercise for reading each other's work helps us to remember, first, that reading is integral to the whole process of writing assignments and is relevant at every stage, and second, that reading does not have to be a solitary activity. Talk about your reading with other students whenever possible; in the long run, doing so will help you to understand more fully what you have read. Other students will have read other things from the same text. Pooling your ideas and thoughts on complicated academic texts can help you make more sense of them. Your ideas will still be your own when you come to write them into your assignment, but sharing them helps you with interpretation.

We hope that by the time you have finished this chapter you will feel less daunted at the idea of reading for your assignments, and will have had the time to experiment with some of the approaches that we suggest. If you have been working through this book from the beginning, you should now have a clear sense of what is involved in the early stages of the process of writing your assignment.

Notes

- Remember to be strategic in your reading for an assignment by establishing what you know already and where you are likely to be going.
- Be discriminating in your reading for an assignment. Remember that making good use of what you know is more important than acquiring a mass of material that you can't digest.
- There is no one right way of reading; the strategies that you adopt and the routes that you take will depend upon the type of reading that you are dealing with.
- It is best to use a quote to support what you have said or are intending to say.
- It is unwise to let the quote do the work for you.
- Remember that reading and writing are an integral part of the same process.

6

Organizing and shaping your writing

Getting the assignment into shape • Different approaches to planning and organizing your writing • Some structures used in university writing • Considering your argument: working out your 'story' and getting your central idea

I can't seem to manage to make a plan before I write my essay.

My tutors are always talking about structure but I'm not sure what this means.

I don't seem to know exactly what I want to say.

My tutors say my writing is muddled.

6.1 Getting the assignment into shape

In this chapter we will be discussing the structure or shape of your assignment – how it is organized. We are assuming that you have already done a lot of work for your assignment. You have worked on the title and have begun to get a sense of where you will be going, and of your argument. You have gathered together a good deal of information from books, lectures and other relevant sources. You have done various kinds of preparatory writing. You may have made some kind of plan and have done pieces of various kinds of writing towards the assignment. But now, probably with the deadline looming, you wonder how you are going to get it into shape as a finished product to hand in to your tutor.

It is true that this can be a very difficult point for the writer. However, we think that if you go through the work we have suggested in other chapters, this part, getting it into shape, will be easier for you because you will have done a good deal of the ordering already. As we proceed in this chapter, we will consider in more detail what we mean by 'well-shaped' writing, when a lot of different pieces have been put together to make a complete piece.

It is important to realize that planning and shaping your writing happen at different phases in the writing process and in different ways. You continually move back and forth between planning and thinking, as you think new thoughts and write down 'old' ones. As you think and gather information you are also planning and writing bits as you go. Similarly, you can find that even as you are working on a piece that you thought was nearly finished, you realize that you need a bit more information. Sometimes, you may find that you have gone in a slightly different direction from the one you had planned so that now you need to revisit material you have already looked at, or even find some new information. Beware though, this can just be a delaying tactic for not getting on to the next hard phase of completing the assignment, on the grounds that it could always be better. At some point you simply need to make the best of what you have got and just finish this particular piece of work.

6.2 Different approaches to planning and organizing your writing

You may remember that in Chapter 3, we introduced the idea of 'building blocks' as a way of thinking about constructing a piece of writing. We can also compare the 'shaping' process with how a child makes a building with bricks. One child might have some idea of the overall structure she wants but she may have to try out different ways of getting there using different arrangements of bricks. She may start off with no idea at all, yet in the end she gets a building she likes. One child might hesitate a lot as he builds; another may just plunge into it. This illustrates that everybody works differently. You will need to try out different ways of planning and writing to find out what works best for you.

The quotes below illustrate different writers' approaches to planning, organizing and shaping their writing. These writers all have some useful ideas that are worth considering when you are thinking about shaping your own writing.

In practice, you may, of course, vary your approach for different purposes and for different kinds of assignment. As with all aspects of writing, it is a good idea to be aware of different methods and to try them out.

The diver writer (see Figure 6.1)

> For years I was confused about my writing because I simply could not carry out my teachers' instructions to 'make a plan' and they were always telling me that my essays should 'be more organized'. I found it very difficult to make an outline and then stick to it. My mind didn't seem to work that way. I always had to start writing and sometimes write quite a lot before I knew where I might be going. That meant I had to cut and do different drafts. Sometimes I would find that I had to start writing one section even if it was in the middle of the assignment, and then build up the whole thing slowly, in bits. In the end it worked out and now I seem to have found my own mix of a method.

This writer just plunges in to her work. She always finds that she has to do some writing before she knows what she wants to say and in order to find out. She might use practice writing (see Chapter 2) for this purpose. Only then can

Figure 6.1 The diver writer

she begin to build up a plan. If she were the child building her house with bricks she would get started and see what kind of building emerged from how she moved around the bricks. She would start to 'just build' her house.

The patchwork writer (see Figure 6.2)

When I write I try to get down some headings that seem to relate to the question. At least they give me an idea of what topics and divisions my writing will have. But I am not yet sure exactly if I have an argument. I start to write what I can under these headings and as I go I am trying to find a way of making these fit together. When I have got my first draft like this I will go back and put in bits that will show the links between the different parts. I may have to move around some material. Sometimes I have to cut out quite a lot because now that I am much clearer about my argument, I realize that not everything I thought was interesting is actually relevant or important. I still have to work out what exactly I have to leave out, add, or move around but gradually I fit the bits together.

Figure 6.2 The patchwork writer

This writer writes sections at an early stage, which she then has to fit together to make the whole assignment, adding links as she goes. If she were the child building a house of bricks she might make a series of different 'rooms' which she would then need to join together to make up the whole house.

The grand plan writer (see Figure 6.3)

I spend a great deal of time reading and making notes – I try to absorb it all thoroughly. I have to read much more than I need. Then I think about it a lot. I can think as I'm doing other things. Finally, I just sit down and write it out in longhand and it's as though it has all come together in my inner mind. Sometimes I add an introduction once I have finished and I will read the whole assignment through, but really I have never found I could write down a plan and my work hardly ever needs redrafting.

Figure 6.3 The grand plan writer

This is a writer who doesn't seem to make an outline at all: she has a 'grand plan' in her 'inner mind'. In fact, she must have a structure in her mind before she begins to write but she can't quite say what it is until she writes it down. Then it comes out nearly complete. The child builder with a grand plan would have a clear picture in her mind of the house she was going to build before she began and would build quickly without getting diverted.

The architect writer (see Figure 6.4)

First I wrote down some notes – ideas for headings. I used the space of a whole page so that I could space out my ideas in a diagram-like fashion. Sometimes I had a column on one side to note down ideas that I might use later on or for jobs I would need to do before I could begin writing the assignment. I kept this list to one side so that I could add to it as I was trying to develop my central overarching idea on the main part of the page. When I had finished I had some notes which all related to this 'central idea' so that I had an outline for the whole piece. Sometimes I like to use visual diagrams for my planning. I think and plan before I even begin to think about starting to write.

The architect writer has a sense of design in her writing. She would not find it too difficult to produce a complex plan. Writers who find it easy to put their thoughts in the form of a spider diagram or mind map are this kind of writer. They have a sense of a broad structure almost before they know what content will go into it, whereas other writers have to know what they have to say

Figure 6.4 The architect writer

before they can make a plan. The 'architect' child building a brick house might start with an outer structure for her building, which she would then fill in to make all her rooms.

What kind of writer are you?

Have you related yourself to one of these types of planning and shaping writing? Try the following activity.

Activity Sixteen: What kind of a 'shaper' are you? How do you plan your writing?

Reread the above descriptions of writers planning their writing. Note down your answers to the following questions:

- What do you think might be the advantages and disadvantages of these different ways of organizing writing?
- Which way of planning and shaping is most like your own approach?
- How do you think your way may be different from any of these?

Now try to describe how you plan and organize your work.

Of course, you may not always adopt just one way of planning and shaping writing. You may in practice adopt different strategies for different kinds of writing that you have to do, and as you get more experience you will find you can become more flexible in your approach.

The writers quoted above demonstrate that the process of shaping their writing is not simple. They all stress that they have found their own way that works for them even if it seems messy and time-consuming. Therefore, although advice on writing an assignment usually emphasizes the need to 'make a plan', these writers, all of whom have some experience, do not follow this advice in any simple way. Some writers do seem to be able to get an outline easily at an early stage, and we suggested one way of working towards this in Chapter 4. There is no doubt that this is useful if you can do it, but, as we have seen, many writers have to do more preliminary thinking or practice writing before they can get a clear structure. However, they do all know that their aim is to get a well-shaped piece of writing in the end.

All this means that there is not just one way to organize a piece of writing. It is important that you do not to try to follow someone else's advice slavishly, because it can dry up your own thought processes. Even when you have been able to plan what you want to say there are often some points in writing an assignment when you don't know what to say next, and most people find that their original plan gets changed as they are writing.

6.3 Some structures used in university writing

Now let us consider the shape of the work from a different angle by looking at some ways of organizing material into different kinds of structure that are commonly used in university writing. By 'structure' we mean both the way a piece of writing is organized and – more importantly – what work it is doing: its function in the assignment. We are particularly interested in how the structure constructs the relationships between different ideas. Here are examples of some structures commonly used in university writing, followed by an illustration of how they might be used for one assignment.

Chronology writing

What happened?

This structure follows time with a sense of the sequence of events, one following another. You *relate* or *recount* what happened. This may, naturally, often be used in history. Chronology can be expressed visually as a 'timeline' which shows the sequence of events during a certain period, as a calendar does. A similar structure may be used to tell the plot of a novel or film. There will often be occasions when you need to use this structure, but you will also need to do more than this and go on to think about and explore further what you have recounted. Chronology writing might well appear at the beginning of an assignment, to give the background to the rest of the piece. Beware of spending too long on chronology writing in any one assignment because the task usually demands more than this.

Description writing

What is something – or someone – like? What are its characteristics or what are the different parts that make it up?

Description usually needs to be followed by or linked to explanation. The visual way to represent description may be as a diagram, with labelled parts, as in biology. However, if we are describing something more abstract – for example, the characteristics of the twentieth-century family – then a spider diagram may be a good way to build up our thinking on what it is like, as we considered in Chapter 2. As with chronology writing, you will usually need to move on to consider more analytic questions, such as why, or what does this mean or what does this relate to.

Cause–effect writing

Why did something happen? What were the consequences?

In practice you will not get far in recounting what happened without bringing in cause and effect, which relate events to each other. Take a simple example: the king died; the people rejoiced. For this to make sense we need to know why the people rejoiced (maybe he was a tyrant). However, the idea of a straight correlation between two events – that something is caused by something else – is often seen as a bit simplistic. All the same, cause and effect – 'what caused something' and/or 'what followed' – can still be an important way of representing a relationship. Of course, as soon as you start to consider 'why' or 'what followed', your thinking becomes complex. How do you know why? What else is involved? Again, you have to analyse many different factors, and usually the first 'why' leads to more questions.

Compare/contrast writing

How are two things different from and like each other?

This is a very common structure. It shows the similarities and differences between two things and, in the process, it tells you more about each of them. One common feature of university writing is that the 'things' may well be quite abstract or intangible – for example, two different social policies or two different psychological theories. You can handle the compare/contrast structure by moving back and forth between both 'things' or by discussing each in turn. This structure might form the main part of your assignment or it may be used for just a part of it. The need for it may well be identifiable in the title of an assignment.

The following kinds of writing are less to do with the way the writing is organized or shaped as with what you are actually doing as you write; in other words, we are concerned with the work that the particular type of organization is doing.

Summary writing

What does the writer say? What is this idea about?

You will sometimes be asked to write a summary and to give the gist of what an article or book is about as an exercise in its own right. You may also have to write briefly about what someone says, or about a particular position or way of thinking as part of your assignment. This is necessary because a lot of university writing is specifically about discussing what other authors have said about a topic. In this case, you will need to refer to just those points and ideas which are relevant to your particular assignment or a specific part of your argument within your assignment. Pointers to summarizing what an author says are given in Chapter 5. Here are some ways in to thinking about summarizing for a particular purpose:

- What is important about what this writer says for your assignment – why do you wish to include something about her/him?
- How do these ideas fit in with what I want to say?

Analysis writing

Going deeper: what is this all about?

This is the most difficult kind of writing to explain because 'analysis' is a term that is frequently used by university tutors in different ways. It always demands that you say more about, for instance, what you are describing or comparing. It requires you to be searching and to ask questions such as:

- What does this mean?
- Why is this important?
- How does this work?
- How is this put together?
- Can you explain this?

These are just some of the questions involved in 'being analytical', or 'using analysis'; use them if they seem appropriate. However, it is equally important to think of your own questions, in context, when you are attempting to be analytical.

Strictly, 'analysis' means breaking things down into their constituent parts, and this idea comes from science. This thought can be helpful in understanding what you need to do in any analytical writing. It means that you can't just make 'big' statements, as you might do in daily life. If you do, tutors might suggest that 'you need to unpack it', to 'tease it out' (we say more about this in the section on feedback in Chapter 11). For example, in film studies students are not required to say whether a film is 'good', which is simply a value judgement, but to work out how it is put together to make its impact. Being analytical involves thinking through what you are doing in your writing and the information and ideas you are presenting in a particular, sharp, questioning way.

Evaluating writing

What is the value of this? How is this important?

In evaluating writing you have to make some sort of a judgement, often about what other writers are saying. This is different from the kind of judgement you might make in daily life, for example, 'That was a good film'. You have to evaluate different positions, perspectives or points of view. You have to do more than say, for example, 'This is a false argument' or 'This is wrong'; you have to give reasons for your judgement.

Evaluating may involve writing about how different positions suggest certain attitudes or omit some crucial information, weighing up one against the other. It is important to remember that in order to evaluate in university writing you have to be analytical. As with all these different kinds of writing, what you actually have to do varies between courses and subject areas, as we elaborated in Chapter 3.

Here is an example of analysis and evaluation from an essay on the 'concept of the family unit' as it is applied to problems of old age:

> There are several disadvantages to using 'the family' as the focus of an explanation for the problems of old age. Firstly, not everyone lives in a family. Secondly, there are now many different forms of families, so generalizations made about the traditional nuclear family are not applicable to all. The consequence of this is that families are expected to behave in ways that do not match reality and they may be blamed for problems connected with old age that they cannot control.

This writer uses analysis in order to evaluate accounts of the problems of old age that are based on the concept of the family unit. You will notice that the analysis is not centrally about the problems of old age but about how these problems are addressed from a particular perspective and position specifically related to the idea of the family unit.

Using a range of writing structures

As we have said, you may well employ more than one kind of writing structure in any one assignment. For example, in the course of writing an account of the causes of homelessness you may have to include a chronological historical account. An assignment about the chronological history of women's writing may also include some analysis of individual works by women writers. Let us take as an example the following assignment: 'Parents have ultimate responsibility for their children's delinquent behaviour. Discuss.'

Chronology writing

You might give a historical account of different attitudes to young offenders; or use a case study in which you recount what happened in a particular case of a young offender.

Compare/contrast

You might want to compare what two writers say on the topic.

Writer A	Writer B
Believes that the family set-up is an important factor in juvenile delinquency.	Believes that factors in society are more important.
Believes that young children can be taught right and wrong at home and school.	Believes that young children cannot be held responsible for their actions.

This would also involve you in some summarizing because you would need to write about what each writer says on the matter. However, you would do this selectively in relation to how you were using the author's work for this assignment (see more about this in Chapter 8).

Analysis writing

In addressing this assignment title you would not (of course) just answer 'yes' or 'no'. You would consider different positions that have been taken on juvenile delinquency and weigh them up. Here is one possible format:

- What are these positions about juvenile delinquency?
- Who holds them and why?
- What attitudes or assumptions about what children are like or about what family life is like do these positions suggest?
- What policies and action follow from them?

As a part of this analysis you will also need to evaluate these different positions and come to some judgement about them.

In this section we have been considering what kind of work your university writing may be doing, which to a large extent determines how it is organized into its shape. Bearing these kinds of structures in mind, both in your reading and your writing, helps you to become more conscious of what you are doing, and so to do it better.

Activity Seventeen: Identifying writing structures

Take one assignment from a subject that you are working on. Can you identify some of the kinds of writing described above that you will need to use in order to answer the assignment? You might find that one kind of writing may shape most of it.

6.4 Considering your argument: working out your 'story' and getting your central idea

One important element of shaping your writing is concerned with developing your argument. An 'argument' is one of the things tutors are most often looking for when they set written assignments, and they often criticize an assignment on the grounds that it does not have an 'argument'. However, in practice, the term often means different things in different subjects and even to different tutors, as we saw in Chapter 3. It certainly doesn't mean a 'quarrel' (although as a matter of fact academics are rather notorious for conducting academic 'quarrels'). An argument can be described in quite technical and particular ways, and we explore this further in the next chapter. Here we are concentrating on developing your central idea and structuring your writing around this.

Building on your central idea step by step

Here is a brief paragraph from the middle of an essay on domestic violence:

> An alternative feminist approach suggests that women may stay in violent relationships even when they are not 'weak'. For these women a constituent of being a woman involves being there for their men and being able to maintain a relationship despite obstacles. These women tried

to understand their violent partners and felt duty bound to cope the best way they could. For them, walking out would have been an admission of failure.

The paragraph contains a common structure on a small scale:

1. *The central idea of the sentence. This is commonly called the 'topic sentence'*: in this case, the 'idea' is a statement about 'an alternative feminist approach'.
2. *Adding to the first idea*: the next sentence gives further explanation about the first statement concerning these women.
3. *An example* of what the women do.
4. A *mini-conclusion* or *summary*.

The writer is extending her central idea, point by point. In practice most paragraphs would build on and extend this basic structure of topic sentence, support, summary/conclusion.

Constructing your 'story'

One way of thinking about developing an argument in your writing is to think of it as your 'story': What is your story? Do you have a clear storyline or plot? Using the notion of a story may not seem very academic, but we think that it gives a good indication of the 'feel' of developing an argument. It should help you to identify more clearly the process of construction that you have to go through to get to a written argument that feels complete for you. Your work as a student writer is to construct your story-argument so that it is convincing to the tutor/reader.

Argument as 'story'

- The story unfolds step by step.
- Selected ideas or events are linked together in an identifiable sequence.
- The reader is given a sense of direction as she reads.
- There is a sense of 'completion' to the whole piece, of it being 'rounded off'.
- There are some predictable patterns and conventions that the writer tries to follow and the reader expects.

Formulating your central idea

In trying to put together your argument it is important to work towards getting the central idea you wish to present. What do you want your reader to know or think by the end of your assignment? What position are you presenting or arguing in this assignment? Or, in the terms we have been considering above, what is your 'story' or storyline? Here are some examples:

There are disadvantages and advantages to the 'care in the community' policy; overall the disadvantages outweigh the benefits.

This advertisement uses signs related to class to try to sell its product.

There are three different theoretical perspectives used to explain domestic violence; they all reveal different attitudes about society.

It is often not easy to formulate this central idea. However, it may be easier if you bear in mind that it needs to form an answer to the assignment title if you have one. If not, the central idea you wish to get over to your reader will help you to think of your own focused title. You may need to do quite a lot of thinking, and even writing, as we have explained, to get to this central idea. You can start to work towards this by analysing the title in the way we suggest in Chapter 4. Once you have been able to sort out your central idea, you will find it easier to shape your assignment because you will be making sure that the information you include is relevant to this central idea. You will know where the writing should be going and have a sense of purpose for it. We must emphasize again that different writers reach the stage of knowing exactly what their assignment is about at different points in their writing. However, it is certainly worth working towards formulating your central idea right from the beginning of your work on any assignment.

A biology student was having difficulty in organizing her short assignment: 'Discuss the membrane as a link and a barrier'. She had many notes and ideas but she couldn't get them into shape. As she put it, 'I can't get my plot'. She meant that she could not yet say, 'The central idea of this assignment is . . .'. Without needing to know anything about the subject, you might think an appropriate shape for this piece of writing could be:

Introduction: what structural features does the membrane consist of?

1. How the membrane functions as a link.
2. How it functions as a barrier.

Conclusion that briefly brings these two aspects together.

But the student couldn't get this to work. As she was talking she suddenly realized that the whole point of what she wanted to say was that the structural features of the membrane worked both as a link and as a barrier at one and the same time. This meant that she had to change her organization as follows:

Introduction: what structural features does the membrane consist of?

1. First structural feature (a) as a link, (b) as a barrier.
2. Second structural feature (a) as a link, (b) as a barrier.

Conclusion that brings these together: that the same things that make the membrane work as a barrier also make it work as a link.

Now she had her 'plot', her central idea, and could get on with the assignment. She felt that there was a much clearer connection between her introduction and the main part of the assignment, and that it made sense. She was able to construct her story-argument.

The idea of an argument as a 'story' may be expressed as follows. The assignment you are writing has a central idea, which expresses what it is about. This central idea is supported by a number of themes, which are organized and linked together into particular structures. The themes may be bits of information, reasons or evidence that make the reader understand and appreciate the central idea. Together these make up the story-argument that you have constructed to answer the assignment most effectively for your purposes.

Developing your argument from topics and themes

We have talked about how an argument is frequently concerned with developing a central idea and the way in which all the different parts of your assignment will be related in some way to this central idea. In your writing you will be concerned with developing a number of themes which support your central idea and therefore provide evidence for the argument that you are making. One way of thinking about the central idea is that it is at the core of your argument. It is the core structure, and building an argument is often about putting together a number of themes to create this core structure. The themes themselves are also made up of components, and these are the basic content-based topics of the assignment. These topics come from your reading and lecture notes and may be concerned with factual material which you need to illustrate and develop your themes. So, in a sense, the topics are the basic building bricks out of which you construct your themes. Remember how we used the analogy of building blocks in Chapter 3. Figure 6.5 illustrates how these topics and themes help to underpin your central idea and support the complete argument.

Look at Figure 6.6, the mind map on 'Famine and its causes'. The student who wrote this used it as the basis of her written assignment. The notes in Figure 5.1 were also hers and relate to the same piece of work. So how would she have gone about putting together her argument? Some of the topics that this student needed to bring in to illustrate her themes can be seen in her mind map: depletion of grain stocks; lack of food; lack of work; cattle prices; migration. From these topics she developed one of her main themes; this was that 'war causes displacement'. She used this, along with other relevant themes, in order to develop her central idea that 'famine was caused by factors other than lack of food'. For her, this idea lay at the heart of the argument that she wanted to express in her assignment. She developed her argument, as she wrote, through the examination of her chosen themes. The argument did not exist before she began to write but it gave voice to the central idea that she wished to develop. Although she had her mind map to guide her, the argument was developed through the writing process as she struggled with the

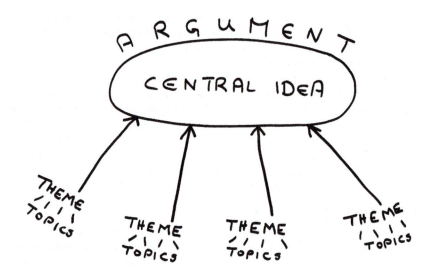

Figure 6.5 Developing an argument

points that she wanted to make at all levels: topics, themes and central idea. The important point to remember is that an argument is not a tangible thing that you can identify somewhere else and import into your assignment. An argument is developed through your writing, and you as the writer make the decision about what weight to give to the different topics and themes that you will be drawing on to build your argument and to express your central idea as clearly as possible to the reader.

Activity Eighteen: Thinking about your central idea

Take an assignment that you are working on or one that you have completed. Write down one or two sentences about what you consider to be the central idea. Write down the topics you will bring in to support your themes. Identify some of the themes that you may write about as part of your argument.

You can save time in organizing and shaping your work by using headings for an outline plan. If you attempt to make an outline plan early on in writing the assignment, then it is useful to make theme headings which you can add to – as much or as little as you like – as you think of new material. Use different sheets of paper for each theme. You can keep these initial notes for as long as you need, as a basis for drafting the whole assignment or for building it up bit by bit.

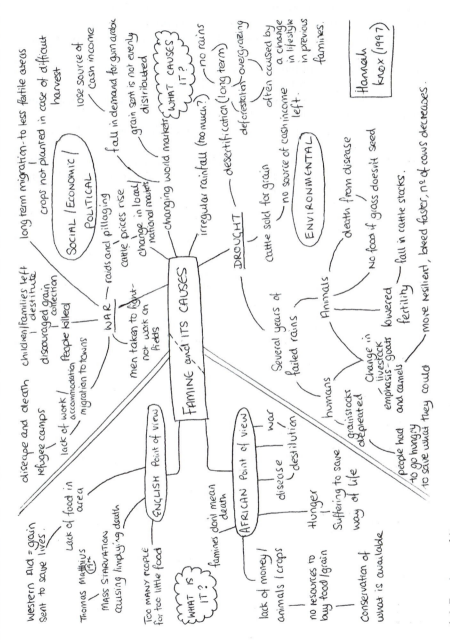

Figure 6.6 Famine and its causes

Notes

- Remember that different writers plan and organize their writing at different stages of the writing process, and try to discover how you work.
- Make a plan if you can but expect to alter it as you write. Always treat your first outline plan as provisional.
- Try to identify how different parts of your writing require a particular structure. To do this, think about what work the writing is doing.
- Above all, determine what your central idea is and make sure that your assignment is organized around this.
- Experiment with mind maps to help you build up the topics and themes for your argument.
- With the computer you can always move things about early on in the planning stage to get an overall feel for how the different parts of your assignment might fit together.

7

Making an argument and persuading your reader*

Your reader • What does 'argument' mean? • How students define 'argument' in their subjects • Developing a thesis statement • Working from first thoughts • Making an argument by anticipating questions and objections • Making an argument by looking at two opposing versions • Persuading the reader

I can't do argument – I'm not the arguing type.

They are always telling me I have to get an argument but they don't explain how to do it.

What do they mean by an 'argument' anyway?

---

* This chapter draws on ideas and material from the thinking writing website at Queen Mary, University of London, (http://www.thinkingwriting.qmul.ac.uk/getstart.htm/ (accessed 7/7/07) and on helpful conversations with Sally Mitchell, co-coordinator of the Thinking Writing Programme.

Activity Nineteen

Before you begin reading this chapter please write down anything at all that you think making an argument might mean in your subject. This will help you to explore and clarify your own thoughts and compare these with what you read in this chapter.

You could do this as notes or in prose, as a piece of practice writing (see Chapter 2).

In the last chapter we looked at different ways of organizing ideas and information in your university writing. We also looked at the need to find a central idea (to get your 'story' or 'plot') and clustering your ideas around this, as a part of building a 'good argument'. In this chapter we continue to explore how to make an argument, but this time with your reader more in the foreground. Putting together an argument is about more than finding a central idea, it also involves making a claim or building up a case and persuading your reader of its worth.

All writing for university needs to be logically organized according to its type; it needs to be coherent and cohesive (see Chapter 11 for more on this) and it needs to be clear for the reader to digest. When you write for university, however, you are often also asked to do more than this: to present a 'good argument'. We call this chapter 'Making an argument and persuading your reader' because we want to suggest that, fundamentally, an argument involves constructing a case through building up a point of view and engaging with those of other people. So, when you make a case in a piece of writing, in a way you are entering into a dialogue, even though it is usually an imaginary one. This takes your writing from a point where you are thinking about how you are handling your information, for instance thinking about what is your main idea and the different ways the writing can be organized in its own terms (as in cause/effect, etc.), to thinking more specifically abut how you can *persuade* your reader to accept the case or claim you are making.

7.1 Your reader

Throughout this book we have thought about your 'reader' as the actual person who will be reading your work: usually your tutor but sometimes another student. Your tutor is usually the person who will be marking your work and who also helps you to develop your ideas and improve your writing, and your fellow student is someone who will be helping you to make your work clearer.

Both of these readers should be interested in what you have to say. In addition, we also talk about you yourself as the reader of your own work.

In this chapter we invite you to think about your reader differently. As well as thinking about your actual reader, we ask you to *imagine* and *construct* a reader progressively as you write, in order to think about how you can build up your case or argument to engage and persuade an actual reader. In the later sections of the chapter, we look at examples of writing that anticipate and deal with how an imaginary reader might respond to the case the writer is trying to build up: the reader who asks questions that make the writer explain and expand on the points they are making, and the reader who puts an opposing point of view. In our final example, which is a piece of academic journalism, we suggest that the author, as he writes, imagines and constructs a reader who is sympathetic to the case he is making. That is, he includes the reader in his writing as someone who would be in agreement with his views.

7.2 What does 'argument' mean?

'Argument' is quite a difficult term when applied to student writing because it is used in many different ways, which we explore below. Sometimes a 'good argument' and a 'good structure' mean the same thing. On the other hand, you can have a good structure in a piece of writing without it strictly being an argument. For example, a large part of a report is exactly that, essentially reporting on something that has been done, or has been found out. Often you may be required to *explain* rather than argue, although your tutors might not make such a distinction.

The requirement to make an argument can also be rather constraining or daunting – as one student said, 'I'm not an argumentative type'. Students who enjoy writing learning journals find that they are often more interested in raising questions, or playing with a range of different ideas, than committing themselves to a particular point of view. And much of a student's work involves analysing different points of view or interpretations before they can think about making their argument.

On the other hand, if you think of making an argument as sorting out what you really want to say, after a good deal of thought and preliminary exploratory writing, then it can become very interesting. In the end, you reach a point where you have something of your own to say, and this is a point at which you find your own 'voice' and a sense of authorship, as we explore in the next two chapters.

We have seen in Chapter 3 that different subjects and even individual tutors have different ideas and expectations about student writing, including their views about argument. It would be a good idea to look back now at what they had to say. The Politics tutor wants students to 'tease out the logic of an argument'. According to the Social Anthropology tutor, social scientists 'use data to support an argument', and the Psychology tutor stresses the need for students to 'pick up on the central issues' and not to put in too much 'description'. The Biology tutor simply asks for the essay to be 'well laid out and well argued'. Most university tutors, then, stress the need to 'get a good argument' and tutors often criticize a student's assignment on the grounds that it does not have an 'argument'. However, as you can tell from what these tutors say, it isn't always easy to know what exactly they mean or what they expect you to do. The idea of what counts as an argument is very different according to the subject of study or discipline. In Chapter 3 we talked about how different subjects view the world though a different 'lens' and how they embody different ideas about what counts as knowledge in a subject. The idea of argument will therefore obviously be different in different subjects.

Sometimes 'getting a good argument', as tutors see it, can be more or less equated with 'thinking critically': taking a questioning approach and thinking about 'Why' or 'So what?' and going beyond the surface of what is described. The sections on analytical reading and the different exercises on reading your own and each other's work in this book are pointers to a critical approach. Throughout the book we always encourage you to think about your own writing in a critical way.

Given these differences then, to begin to find out what getting a good argument in a particular subject might mean in your study, have a look at some guidelines from your department and listen to what your tutors have to say. Reading texts in your subject should also help you to see how the ideas are put together. Reading analytically and critically, as we explained it in Chapter 5, will also help you to build up a sense of how authors develop their ideas.

7.3 How students define 'argument' in their subjects

To find out more about how argument is seen in different subjects we asked some postgraduate students to write brief answers to the question, 'What does "argument" mean in your subject?' We asked these students because they are quite experienced writers in their subject, they have recently been undergraduates themselves, and are now thinking hard about what it means to become an authority in their subject. As you will see, their ideas and ways of writing about argument demonstrate how different subjects present the world and make knowledge differently. At the same time, there were common themes in what they said:

- argument as a piece of writing that is 'coherent' with its parts clearly connected to each other, what many call a 'logical flow';

- argument as the presentation of a case, or as examining 'both sides' of a case;
- argument as logically connected writing;
- argument as a 'thesis' with supporting evidence and reasons.

These general points are a useful basis for you to think about argument in your own writing.

It is interesting to compare the tutor comments in Chapter 3 with what the students thought: the tutors talked about 'what I look for in a student's essay' while the students are trying to work out for themselves what they need to do and how their subject works.

Below are some examples of what the students wrote. Please note that these are just examples of what individual students who were thinking about their own work had to say. They are interesting and useful for you to think about and to compare with each other but are not to be taken as standardized directions for how to write.

Psychology: two students

I mostly think of argument when I write essays with the word 'discuss' in it. Then we are expected to take one side of the argument and provide relevant evidence and then take the other side of the argument. We are discouraged from writing about arguments in lab reports because it becomes too opinionated and it is merely meant to be a report and study of a specific experiment.

This student points out that 'argument' is only relevant in some situations. In others, it is a question of just reporting or sometimes 'explaining' rather than 'making a case'.

From my experience of reading psychological journals, much time is spent on replicating past studies and a means for validating or refuting past conclusions. These experimenters then use 'hard' evidence to strongly defend their personal perspectives and fight off arguments presented by other researchers within the similar field.

Here, argument is seen as a kind of contest between two opposing sides who have to be 'fought off', which is more like the everyday sense of the term.

History

The idea of argument or thesis is quite central to my subject's rationale for its own evidence; interpretation and engagement with the work of others is widely viewed as the heart of the distinction between 'history' and 'antiquarianism'. Most historians would say that a work's argument should be explicit and should have a central thread upon which the rest of the content should hang, although how often they follow this instruction is perhaps open to question.

Notice this writer's uncertainty about how far 'this instruction' to 'have a central thread' is actually followed. Sometimes tutors may give their students advice that they do not follow themselves. This is partly because often an argument does not present itself fully formed to the reader or even to the writer but has to be built up in the course of writing. It may also be because writers may be doing other things in the course of their writing. In the case of history, for example, they can spend time recounting, constructing a story of 'what happened'.

History/Philosophy

Constructing an argument for a historical piece of work is somewhat different from an argument for a philosophical piece. Let's say that an argument in both disciplines is logically derived from a premise and the same goes for a negation of the thesis. However, history is confined to the available sources whereas philosophy rather depends on the logical representation.

This student compares their experience of writing history and philosophy and suggests that 'supporting a premise' may be quite different in the two disciplines. They suggest that philosophy relies on reasoning and logic, history more on what is known already.

Biological physics

In my subject, argument means the ability to create a believable theory, which is supported by hard data. I imagine this is easier than other disciplines because it is easier to defend yourself when you are backed up by quantifiable repeatable results. It can also be more difficult as you have to place your argument in the context of previous work and results, which may contradict those which you find. Argument is never directly personal. Argument is purely a process of translating specific data into a reasonable scenario (consistent with known phenomena).

This student compares the 'evidence' of science with other subjects and also stresses how the subject is meant to be impersonal.

Law

An argument is an answer to a question – in law it often concerns a normative opinion that one must agree or disagree with (or a part thereof) and justify that agreement or otherwise. It involves typically an analysis of an area of law that says what it is, how it is. At the end you have to state your opinion but never develop an original position.

The statement that you must 'never develop an original position' is interesting and might come as a surprise to students working in some other disciplines.

Sciences

Summarizing the diversity of corroborating or opposing theories or experimental data on a particular topic; discussing which author agrees with who, and if they disagree, on what grounds – data or interpretation. You need to be as balanced as possible in your presentation of the two or more sides before probably summing up the essence of the argument (or main points of contention) and declaring which you find most convincing. In science, you need to be balanced but not in law.

Note that this student claims to be able to speak for sciences in general and to compare sciences with law. However, this view is different from that of the law student, above, who writes about the academic study of law. This science student seems to refer to a court of law where a barrister has to try to persuade a jury by using a mix of fact and persuasion. This view of argument as making and trying to win a case through persuasive argument is nearer to our everyday meaning of 'having an argument', as well as what goes on in courts of justice. Although the idea of making a strong case also often underlies academic writing requirements, the writer is always expected to be 'balanced' in presenting different viewpoints even when she or he ends up on one side.

This student went on to introduce a sense of argument that is more like a 'story' (as we suggest in Chapter 6):

Presenting your material in a particular sequence – perhaps in a historical piece detailing the development of a theory or resolution of a controversy, e.g. Darwinian selection in 1860s to 1880s.

Another science student wrote about argument as 'the journey of your essay', with a 'logical flow' and a 'thread of a sort between parts'. Yet another wrote in an amusing way about how scientists are supposed to build on others' work to make a new claim:

I would say that an 'argument' in science has to reflect both sides: while Vile and Calumny 1996 say that so and so happens, Veracity and Truth 1998 say that this and that happens. Our results agree with Veracity and Truth but extend the boundaries of their supposition. In the Ideal World, the scientific argument would be an evidence-based rationale, i.e. '. . . from what we have found out and from what we already know, then we think that the following is happening.'

However, argument is now driven by hypothesis, and so has become more subjective, i.e. '. . . from what we already know we have the following idea. We will perform a series of experiments that we believe will give evidence to the support of that idea.'

Finally, there is the popular definition of argument – an altercation. This is usually conducted via publications, utilizing refutations and counter-refutations (a lengthy process but polite), or at meetings (which is usually a shorter and more brutish process).

Here we see the familiar statement that a student writer needs a strong idea with supporting evidence. This statement ends by referring back to the 'popular' idea of argument as a 'quarrel', mockingly suggesting that academics also engage in this kind of argument.

English

The argument of an essay in English Literature need not necessarily make or rehearse an argument for or against a particular position or inter- pretation, though it might do this – it might attempt to make a case for a new reading, or demolish an existing piece of criticism. Very good literary- critical essays can be primarily analytical and descriptive, demonstrating how a particular piece of writing works, or how a writer thinks or feels; but an essay of this type would still need a coherent structure, a clear connection of its materials and a consequentiality (one thing following another) in the remarks made about them. This discursive movement might be called an argument, although it would not necessarily be argu- mentative; so that 'argument' is perhaps just the word conventionally used about a critical essay where one would use 'form' about a literary work. From another angle, and on the analogy of the prose 'Arguments' prefixed to each book of *Paradise Lost*, one might say that the argument of an essay is a statement of its paraphrasable content, a summary or abstract, a narrative reduction. To answer the question 'What is your argument?' would thus entail telling a little story about the material you proposed to discuss and the position you took towards it.

This English student points to his belief that writing about literature is quite different from other disciplinary writing. Yet, the need to make a case is still strongly present. The idea of argument as 'story' makes an appearance here too.

Linguistics

The term argument I feel is used very briefly in linguistics for a very broad range. For example, each paragraph in an essay needs to be its own argument in the whole essay, which is an argument itself. Within an argument evidence from other linguists is needed, often empirical evidence or citations from other linguists is needed but both sides need to be presented.

Critically an argument must give both sides of the coin and argue for which you believe using empirical evidence. In linguistics you must be able to show the various ideas people have about certain subjects such as morphosyntax and morphology and be able to explain and critique both, arguing within the explanation for and against the ideas. Argument is a very complex idea.

The linguistics student notes the complexity of the idea of argument. At the same time, for this student both writing and building up an argument is a very systematic process with the observation that each paragraph can, in itself, be a mini argument.

Activity Twenty

Now that you have read these comments, look back at what you have written for Activity Nineteen about an argument in your own subject (or one of the subjects you are studying) and then compare your own thinking with what these students have to say. You may now want to add to your own thoughts.

7.4 Developing a thesis statement

When you make an argument you are making a case for a particular point of view that you want your reader to accept. You are taking a particular stance on a subject and often make a *claim* about it. As we stressed in Chapter 6, and as your tutors will usually tell you, this involves formulating a central idea and organizing your material around this to support it, so that you can justify your claim. A common term for the 'central idea' is a 'thesis statement', which points more to developing an argument to persuade the reader. Writing a simple thesis statement can be a useful way of signalling to the reader – and to yourself – that you have a central argument that the whole essay will build on. It clarifies what you are doing and serves as a guide to the essay. As always, though, there are differences between subjects, and using an explicit thesis statement is more common in some than others. In the last chapter (see, for instance, the section on topic and themes) we look at how your whole piece of writing – and the thinking that goes into it – can all together make up your 'argument'.

Perhaps the greatest advantage to you as a writer in developing a thesis statement is that it puts your own thinking into your essay. Instead of just describing what others have to say, for example, you have put your own thinking to work. You have to make your own sense of your material in order to come to your own conclusion. Having a thesis statement means you are putting your own, unique mark on your essay. By the time you have sorted out your central thesis you will have worked your way through your material to your own conclusion.

Making a thesis statement shows that you have decided on how you want your essay to deal with your chosen topic, or how it is handling a topic that you yourself have chosen. It shows that you have come to see your topic in terms of a problem to be solved or an issue you have to think through; and that you have come to a definite position on it. Once you can get to this point you will have got past simply writing descriptively, and certainly beyond just writing down all you know about a subject. Arriving at a thesis statement is therefore something that is really useful to aim at in your thinking. From your reader's point of view, too, having a thesis statement makes understanding and then assessing your essay much easier. It also suggests that you are making a case for your particular point of view about a topic and that you have managed to channel a mix of material and ideas into this single guiding idea. Once you have your thesis statement, you will be able to think about how each paragraph contributes towards adding to, explaining or proving the thesis.

Usually, a thesis statement is preceded by what we might call a 'statement of intent' – a short introduction. As an example, this is how we could have introduced this chapter on 'Making an argument':

> In this chapter we will address the notion of 'argument' in student writing. We will attempt to make the idea of 'argument' more accessible by analysing various ways it is seen in academic writing and we will relate it to the idea of a central 'thesis statement'. To illustrate disciplinary difference we will look at what students on different courses have to say about argument. There are many ways of conceiving argument in student writing, depending on the discipline.

7.5 Working from first thoughts

Making an argument means, at some point, and in some way, you have something to say that you want to put over to your reader. You arrive at the position of taking your own stance and putting forward your point of view about a subject. In academic writing this is normally based on evidence or reasoning, including your own use of relevant and appropriate sources. This is something we discuss in the next chapter. Often issues are not clear-cut and you will have to acknowledge this. However, most academic work does end up by making a claim even though this might emerge slowly as you develop your case.

Very often a student essay has to answer a question. At first glance this can draw an immediate response, either positive or negative. For example, keeping within the theme of the family, the response to the question 'Does marriage encourage family stability?' might be either: 'Marriage encourages family stability' or 'Marriage does not encourage family stability'. Obviously, these are very strong assertions that you would rarely expect to find in academic writing, which would be more circumspect; for example, 'A recent study suggests that families with married parents are more stable than those of unmarried parents'. This less dogmatic statement is also open to questioning since different types of research could probably be found to support or oppose it. The question of marriage and family stability does not have definitive answers. It also illustrates tensions between everyday understandings about 'the family' in contrast to more specific, academic meanings. It raises issues such as:

- What sort of information – facts – are you drawing on here? This would come from your reading (or if you were a researcher from your research). Individual experience might also be brought to bear on the question. For example, if you were brought up by a single parent you would have own views that might influence your initial response.
- How do we define 'family stability'? Before we address that question, we might want to think about: How do we define a 'family'? (For examples, look back at our ideas about how different disciplines define 'family' in Chapter 2.)
- Underlying these sorts of rational or logical questions are other questions to do with individual and society's values: for example, marriage has specific value from a religious point of view.
- Finally, once these kinds of questions have been thought through, there could be further questions about any actions that might be appropriate in thinking about this issue – e.g. on how to support families, married or not.

So there are different kinds of possible perspectives, to do with *facts, definitions, values, action* – all of which need to be taken into account when preparing to write about a topic. The particular course you are doing will guide your approach to these.

7.6 Making an argument by anticipating questions and objections

One useful way of thinking about argument is in terms of having a conversation with your imagined reader. This conversation might be in terms of a dialogue, for example, a series of responses to questions or objections that a reader could make.

Activity Twenty-one

Now apply this idea to the paragraph below by considering possible questions, objections and counter-arguments from an imaginary reader.
    Read the paragraph (taken from Chapter 6), note down any questions or objections each sentence raises for you as you read, and then compare them with our comments below.

> An alternative feminist approach suggests that women may stay in violent relationships even when they are not 'weak'. For these women a constituent of being a woman involves being there for their men and being able to maintain a relationship despite obstacles. These women tried to understand their violent partners and felt duty bound to cope the best way they could. For them walking out would have been an admission of failure.

Commentary

Here are our ideas about how a reader might respond:

An alternative feminist approach suggests that women may stay in violent relationships even when they are not 'weak'.

> Reader: What is this feminist approach? Where have you read about this? Please explain this more to me.

This suggests that the writer may need to cite some sources to back up the statement and expand on it; see Chapter 8 for more on this.
    Still on the first sentence, the reader might say:

> Reader: That seems very strange. I just don't understand why women would ever stay in a violent relationship.

However, as if to anticipate this objection, the following sentence of the paragraph takes this question into account and explains:

For these women a constituent of being a woman involves being there for their men and being able to maintain a relationship despite obstacles.

And we might imagine that the writer in conversation with the reader could add: *So maybe these women have a different idea of their relationship and marriage from the one you are assuming is the case.* This suggests how the writer might have to find out and write more about this, in expanding the paragraph. For the moment, the reader may still not be convinced:

> Reader: But surely it is still a weakness to stay with a man who is violent? Surely feminists think that women should be strong and not let men exploit them? I still don't understand how staying can be a sign of strength.

The writer's next sentence is an attempt to explain things further: *These women tried to understand their violent partners and felt duty bound to cope the best way they could. Walking out would have been an admission of failure.*

This series of imagined exchanges suggest that as a writer making an argument you always have to anticipate and take into account questions and counter-arguments that you can imagine a reader putting forward.

7.7 Making an argument by looking at two opposing versions

When you make an argument for a reader it may be important to consider how the reader might oppose your argument. You may do this in your writing by looking at two opposing accounts and arguing for the one you think is the stronger, as in the student essay in Activity Twenty-two below.

Activity Twenty-two

Read the following extracts from a short student essay called 'Why was Socrates put on trial?' Note how it presents two opposing versions for the reasons for Socrates' trial, the 'official' version, and the writer's alternative version.

Why was Socrates put on trial?
The official charges on which Socrates was tried were impiety and corrupting the youth. Meletus, his chief accuser, claimed that Socrates was subversive, undermining the authority of the state and its Gods with his unorthodox

philosophizing. Furthermore, he encouraged other young citizens to follow his example with disrespectful questioning of established truths and figures.

However, as Socrates states in his defence, it is not logically possible for him to be impious. He cannot believe in divine actions and not believe in divinities; this is a contradiction. He frequently refers to his own 'God' [and . . .] Socrates always participated in the city's religious ceremonies. Also it is not sensible to accuse Socrates of knowingly corrupting the youth. This is based on the assumption that no intelligent person would ever wish to corrupt those around them because, among other things, they would be causing themselves harm. Either he does not corrupt them at all or he does so unwittingly.

Socrates clearly was not put on trial for these reasons alone. The motives of those responsible for the trial of Socrates were not documented in the official charges. It was rather the controversy that Socrates aroused and the instability that this threatened that caused his trial. Athens having just recovered from the prolonged war with Sparta, in which they were defeated, was a very delicate democracy. A man with as much influence as Socrates was too dangerous to keep within a community that was struggling to rebuild itself.

The reasons for Socrates' trial therefore cannot be confined to any acts of civil disobedience that he may or may not have been guilty of, but rather the convincing way in which his philosophical attacks (which he considered to be innocent) destabilized an already fragile society, fearful of further disintegration and unrest.

The essay sets up one line of argument and then shows how this is opposed by another, which the writer goes on to argue is the 'correct' view.

You could imagine this writing being based on a dialogue, as if the reader is involved at each point, almost at each sentence. It is as if the writer is anticipating and encouraging the reader to question the first argument. The writing proceeds in a series of 'moves' that act as if to include the reader in the exploration and construction of the argument, by allowing them to comment and ask questions. Below, after each section, we have inserted what we imagine a reader could have said in response; the writer then writes as if anticipating these responses.

Why was Socrates put on trial?

The official charges on which Socrates was tried were impiety and corrupting the youth. Meletus, his chief accuser, claimed that Socrates was subversive, undermining the authority of the state and its Gods with his unorthodox philosophizing. Furthermore, he encouraged other young citizens to follow his example with disrespectful questioning of established truths and figures.

Reader: You say 'official' charges. I suppose that this means there were 'unofficial' reasons that you will tell us about? Do you mean that the official reasons were not the real reasons?

However, as Socrates states in his defence, it is not logically possible for him to be impious. He cannot believe in divine actions and not believe in divinities; this is a contradiction. He frequently refers to his own 'God' [and . . .] Socrates always participated in the city's religious ceremonies. Also it is not sensible to accuse Socrates of knowingly corrupting the youth. This is based on the assumption that no intelligent person would ever wish to corrupt those around them because, among other things, they would be causing themselves harm. Either he does not corrupt them at all or he does so unwittingly.

Reader: So, since you are suggesting that Socrates was a great and intelligent philosopher only concerned with getting at the truth (and you assume that your reader would agree with that), who would not want to harm anyone, then you want us to agree that, of course, these charges were false. So I see what you are about to say . . .

Socrates clearly was not put on trial for these reasons alone.

Reader: No, of course not. Obviously, as your reader I agree with your 'clearly'. So what were the *real* reasons?

The motives of those responsible for the trial of Socrates were not documented in the official charges. It was rather the controversy that Socrates aroused and the instability that this threatened that caused his trial. Athens having just recovered from the prolonged war with Sparta, in which they were defeated, was a very delicate democracy. A man with as much influence as Socrates was too dangerous to keep within a community that was struggling to rebuild itself.

Reader: Oh I see. As you suggested at the beginning, there were other reasons for his trial. But I don't understand quite why he was considered 'dangerous'?

The reasons for Socrates' trial therefore cannot be confined to any acts of civil disobedience that he may or may not have been guilty of, but rather the convincing way in which his philosophical attacks (which he considered to be innocent) destabilized an already fragile society, fearful of further disintegration and unrest.

Reader: Oh I see, so there might have been a bit of truth in the 'official' reason but that certainly wasn't the real reason he was put on trial. Obviously, no city in that situation can put up with being undermined. Thank you for explaining it so clearly!

This essay sets out the 'official' position for the trial. It goes on to refute this position and ends with a statement that sums up the writer's claim to know the truth about this question.

Here we have been imagining a reader who tries to understand what you want to say and it is always worth thinking about different kinds of readers, those you can imagine as well as the actual reader – who will be the tutor who also marks your essay. In the next section we see how a writer imagines and then constructs the 'reader' of his work, as a means of persuasion.

7.8 Persuading the reader

We have been suggesting throughout this chapter that making an argument is about having a position on a topic and engaging the reader – in the end, it is about persuading the reader to adopt your point of view or position. We have been looking at ways of making the argument with the reader in mind and in this final section we look in more detail at how the reader can be persuaded of the author's point of view. Interestingly, this piece of writing persuades not by imagining the reader as an adversary but as someone who is already prepared to sympathize with the author's own position.

The piece of writing we are going to consider in Activity Twenty-three is not conventionally 'academic'; for example, it has no references and it is polemical. This article is best described as a piece of academic journalism; it is about higher education and the author is a professor of higher education. The piece was first published in *The Times Higher Education Supplement* (*THES*), a UK weekly newspaper for those concerned with higher education policy and practice. We have chosen it as a good example of writing that progressively involves and persuades the reader by using language in particular ways in order to build a powerful argument.

Activity Twenty-three

- Read through the article. Consider the following questions, which we discuss in our notes below.
- First note down your initial responses. For example: What does it make you think or feel? Do you feel engaged or not by it?
- What does its central idea seem to be? Is this actually expressed in one or two sentences? Can you grasp this from the beginning?
- Do you find yourself persuaded by the article?
- What do you think the writer wants you to believe?

- What kinds of supporting evidence does it use?
- Where and how does the article draw on an assumption of shared understanding or agreement in its reader?
- What effect does the use of 'I' have on you as reader?

We have numbered the paragraphs of this article – some of which are very short – in order to help with the discussion which follows.

1. A love of knowledge, the most valuable resource of Universities UK, is being squandered by policies designed for the marketplace.

2. A colleague who bubbles with enthusiasm for his subject recently told me he was taking early retirement. When asked why, he said, 'So that I can pursue my studies'. When I retold this story to a number of others, they sympathized. Whether a university is the best, or even a good, place for intellectual pursuit seems to be in question. And if it is in question for staff, will it not soon be in question for students?

3. The negative consequences of accountability will be familiar to anyone who reads *THES*. They include requirements that research proposals should detail the outcomes of research before it has even begun; that publication should be in forms and timescales that suit assessment exercises; that teaching should be conducted in ways that ensure its outcomes are predictable; that trails of paper should document every decision; and that increasing effort should be put into reports (and

reports on the reports) of academic work, at the expense of academic work itself.

4. As a result, not only does the academic have increasingly little time to teach or research, but a culture has developed which lacks trust and is fearful of risk. Students become reluctant to learn anything that does not translate directly into improved exam grades; staff are encouraged to teach only in ways that maximize 'satisfaction' ratings from their 'customers'; and research is driven by a lust for publication lists and funding rather than a love of knowledge.

5. Government policies have reflected a view that higher education which is pursued out of a search for truth may have been alright for the scholarly elites of a few cloistered institutions, but not appropriate to the masses which modern higher education serves. Such a view is narrow-minded and patronizing to a public that is assumed to have little interest in the pursuit of knowledge. If the next generation of graduates is to address the problems of our increas-

ingly complex global society, their curiosity and critical faculties need to be nurtured and directed toward the common good. Skills training for employment does not, on its own, provide a sufficient justification for a higher education.

6. The old dichotomy between employment *versus* knowledge for its own sake should be abandoned. In the longer term, the prospects for a prosperous as well as a more civilized society will be best served by valuing knowledge and the curiosity – with its associated risks – that is characteristic of the best students and staff.

7. So what policies do I recommend?

8. First, the sector appears to be tired of new initiatives and funding arrangements in competition for resources. A disproportionate amount of energy is spent administering and accounting for small, ring-fenced, funds and too much time has been spent learning games in order to maximize chances of success in relation to research and teaching. Government needs to hold back on new initiatives in

order to provide a breathing space for higher education.

9. Second, there should be fewer, simpler systems of accountability that give prominence to qualitative professional judgement rather than the spurious measurements which inevitably lead to game-playing.

10. Third, curricula and research which emphasize genuine exploration, particularly across disciplinary, professional and other cultural boundaries, should be encouraged at all levels, acknowledging that risk and the possibility of failure are an inevitable part of innovation in an uncertain world.

11. Finally, government should start a wider public debate on the purposes of higher education, in which the economic are related to the wider cultural benefits of a more educated public. Higher education has changed radically over the last 30 years in response to the market, but these changes have not been the consequence of public or academic debate. To achieve this, intellectual leadership is required rather than managerial accounting.

12. But such changes to policy will come to nothing unless the higher education community contributes imaginatively to this debate. Too ready to comply with, and then complain about the consequences of, government impositions, academics have been reluctant to explain the value of their work.

13. Leaders of institutions have let us down. Protesting the excellence of their own institutions, they have said little about their purposes or those of the sector as a whole, and how these relate to the needs of society. Mission statements and strap lines have come to replace serious thinking about what universities are for, rather than be a distillation of that thinking. The sector needs to be much more courageous in setting out its stall.

14. A system of higher education which celebrates a love of knowledge in pursuit of the common good would involve all academics in such debate. And students too. Now that would be real accountability.

(Rowland, S (2007) Now then what am I meant to be doing here? *Times Higher Educational Supplement,* June 2007)

In the first sentence (1) a strong and potentially contentious claim, that could be considered the thesis statement for the article, is made: '*A love of knowledge . . . is being squandered by policies designed for the marketplace'*. The article will have to provide support for the statement. The phrase, '*the most valuable resource of Universities UK'*, is also a claim but is slipped in as if it is a fact that the reader is bound to accept. It is expressed as a shared assumption that expects you, as a reader of this newspaper, to agree with.

Paragraph 2 begins with the statement about '*A colleague . . . taking early retirement so that "I can pursue my studies"'*. We are told that '*others sympathized'*. These two sentences are offered as evidence or rather as an illustration of that strong first claim. As 'evidence' it would be weak; we do not even know that the 'colleague' spoke the words given. It is anecdotal evidence, which the reader has simply to accept is true. The writer appears to assume that many of his readers – and certainly the reader he imagines – would agree with what the 'colleague' says. So the anecdote serves to include the reader in this way of thinking.

The next two paragraphs, 3 and 4, support the central claim that a love of knowledge is being squandered by policies for the marketplace with examples of what is happening in universities. The writer's main job at this point is to make a case to support the phrase '*policies designed for the marketplace'*.

In paragraph 3, '*Accountability*' is used as a pejorative term to suggest '*policies designed for the work place*'. Some people might think that accountability was a good thing but the examples given here strongly refute any 'good' aspect and focus on ways in which accountability destroys a '*love of the subject*' and how it is just about the '*marketplace*'.

In paragraph 4, the language becomes increasingly more polemical: staff are '*reluctant to take risks*' (by implication 'risks' are a good thing); '*students become reluctant to learn*'; teaching becomes a transaction between '*customer*' and seller. Notice, too, that a dichotomy is set up between '*lust for publication*' and the '*love of knowledge*'.

Paragraph 5 refers back to paragraph 1, claiming that government policies have reflected a particular view of HE (that the pursuit of truth is not appropriate to the masses); and also that this view is '*patronizing and narrow*'. Note that in this paragraph the '*love of truth*' is equated with '*pursuit of knowledge*'. If the reader were to question this, the central idea of the argument could be challenged.

Notice too the suggestion that '*the pursuit of truth*' is not suitable for the '*masses*' is immediately countered by the statement '*the curiosity and critical faculties of the next generation needs to be nurtured and directed towards the common good*'. It is as if the writer has set up a rather exaggerated counter-argument only in order to claim that it is mistaken, that '*it is narrow-minded and patronizing*'.

The next paragraph (6) contains two more claims written in just two sentences: '*The old dichotomy between employment and knowledge for its own sake should be abandoned.*' The idea that there is such a dichotomy has been set up already in the previous paragraph. The next sentence gives a further reason for the reader to agree with the claim: '*the prospects for a prosperous as well as a more civilized society will be best served by valuing knowledge and the curiosity that is characteristic of the best students and staff*'.

So by now there has been a movement from the claim that the love of knowledge is being squandered to a claim that it should instead be '*nurtured*'. This concludes the first section of this 800-word piece of writing.

In paragraph 7, the author uses 'I' to assert his right to recommend new policies. Each of the four recommendations is signalled to the reader clearly as a numbered list in paragraphs 8–11. Each recommendation, to '*hold back on new initiatives*'; have '*fewer systems of accountability*', '*genuine exploration*', '*a wider public debate with intellectual leadership*' is based on the assumption that the reader will be in agreement with the claim that knowledge and curiosity should be valued in HE.

Paragraph 12 qualifies these last four recommendations and, having urged the government to change, now turns back and urges the same of academics. Suddenly, the writer seems to be attacking academics: Academics have been '*too ready to comply*', have '*been reluctant*' to object. In paragraph 13, the leaders of academic institutions are criticized in even stronger terms than the government with a new claim, '*Leaders of institutions have let us down*'. Here, *'us'* includes the reader who has come to agree with what has been said. This claim is supported by a series of points which back up the idea that *'leaders of institutions have let us down'*.

The final paragraph (14) offers a change in the meaning of *'accountability'*: at the beginning of the piece accountability was equated with the *'marketplace'*. Now *'real'* accountability celebrates a *'love of knowledge'*, which is now – having got rid of the *'dichotomy'* between *'employment and knowledge'* – presented as *'for the common good'*. The common good involves everyone, including all the readers who by now, the article assumes, agree with all that has been argued.

So, in this article the author uses anecdote, assertions and claims, and strong language both to bring himself into the piece, and to include the reader in the process of building his argument. It makes strong claims in simple, short sentences and clear, accessible language.

Although this is obviously not an academic essay, nevertheless, it is a well-argued piece of writing about the aims and purposes of higher education for an educated and well-informed reader that can help us in thinking about making an argument. It demonstrates how writing can be used rhetorically to persuade a reader. This is something that you might well be asked to do for different kinds of assignments during your studies (see Chapter 12).

Making an argument is about the process of sorting out what you really want to say, after a good deal of thought and preliminary, exploratory writing. When you use writing to make a claim, and to engage your reader, you will find that you are getting closer to the 'strong argument' that your tutors often ask for. You will become the owner of your ideas and will find your own voice and a sense of authorship of your university writing, as we explore further in Chapter 9. Before that, in the next chapter, we look at how you can use a wide range of sources as a basis for developing your own argument.

Activity Twenty-four: Imagining your reader

Think of a topic that you have strong views and feelings about. Now imagine your reader as someone who is always interested in whatever you might have to say. This might be an actual person or you may create an imaginary reader. Write quickly to this person expressing your position about the topic.

Now read over what you have written.

Could you make use of the persuasive ways of writing illustrated in the article above in order to engage your reader more effectively?

Notes

- Remember that argument has very different meanings in different subjects.
- Try to trace how authors in your field of study build up their arguments.

- Work towards getting a 'thesis' for your argument but don't necessarily expect to get there straight away.
- Think of argument as a conversation with a reader where you deal with questions and disagreements to persuade your reader of the strength of your own case.

8

Making good use of your sources

Referencing systems • Referencing websites • Referencing other sources • Recording references • Referencing and plagiarism • Thinking about plagiarism • Using your sources creatively

Do I need to reference it even if I heard it in one of my lectures?

I'm really scared about plagiarizing by mistake.

Do you have to put in a date if you use something from the Internet?

In this chapter we look at the different resources that you might be using in your university writing. Whatever course you are studying and whatever the level of study, you are likely to find yourself drawing from a wide range of sources in writing your assignments. Until a few years ago you would have probably found these within the four walls of the university library but changes in both accessing information and in what counts as knowledge during the last decade mean that students now draw on sources from a wide range of contexts. Whatever these might be, you will always be expected to reference everything very meticulously, including not just conventional books and journal articles and of course the Internet but also sources from lectures or personal communication, such as email. In this chapter we consider the range of sources that you may be using and how to reference these in your assignments; we then go on to discuss plagiarism and how understanding more about using your sources not only helps you to avoid plagiarism but can also help you develop your own voice in your writing.

There are now many websites which discuss the issues around plagiarism and using sources; these complement this chapter and can provide you with up-to-date guidance. Many universities also have their own guidance available online about avoiding plagiarism and at the time of writing we found two that were particularly useful:

- http://turnitin.com/research_site/e_home.html Turnitin Research Resources (accessed 17/07/07)
- http://www.yale.edu/bass/writing/sources/index.html Yale University, The Writing Centre (accessed 17/07/07)

Our first task is designed to help you to consider the range of different sources you might use in writing your assignments.

Activity Twenty-five: Looking at your sources

Take an example of one or two of your own written assignments. (If this is your first term at university you may need to use something you wrote and had assessed before you came to university.)

Now make a list of all the different types of resources you have used in these assignments.

Do you know how to cite these different sources in your assignment writing?

These are some of the sources that we have seen students and academics using. How many of these have you listed?

Books
Articles
Book chapters
Government reports
Newspaper reports
Other kinds of reports
Internet sources
Online journals (without a print version)
Online versions of print journals (usually a downloadable pdf document that can then be treated as hard copy)
Articles found online (not in journals)
Websites of organizations and private individuals
Blogs
Forums, chats, discussion boards, list servs
Lectures
Personal correspondence (e.g. email, personal communication with your tutor)

If you feel unsure about how to reference any of these sources, then you should pay close attention to any guidance that you have been given by your department or the university more generally. You can also ask your tutor or look at some of the websites we list at the end of this book. We discuss some examples of ways of referencing below.

8.1 Referencing systems

There are two main referencing systems in use in universities. One of these uses a numbering system in the text with notes at the end of the chapter or article; this system often also uses extensive footnoting, and a bibliography is included of works that have been used during the writing of the text. The alternative system that we illustrate below is called the Harvard system; its use is widespread across many different academic fields of study. In this system, the author's name and the date of publication are given in parentheses in the text and refer to a section at the end of the publication, headed 'References', which in turn contains details of all the published works that have been referenced. We use this system in this book. The Harvard system looks like this:

References
Fairclough, N. (1992) *Discourse and Social Change*. London: Polity Press.
Heath, S.B. (1982) What no bedtime story means: narrative skills at home and at school, *Language in Society*, 11(1): 49–76.
Lea, M. and West, L. (1995) Motives, mature students, the self and narrative, in J. Swindells (ed.) *The Uses of Autobiography*. London: Taylor & Francis, pp. 128–146.

As you will see, it is always the name of the published volume which is italicized (or sometimes underlined or emboldened), whether it is a single author book, an edited volume or a journal. References include the names of the authors in the order in which they appear on the title page; the date of publication; the title of the book, article or journal (as appropriate); the place of publication and the publisher. If you are quoting from a chapter in an edited volume or an article in a journal you also need to record the page numbers. Although there may be some slight variations in punctuation conventions, these key details are always present in the final list of references. What is most important in referencing is consistency: all your references must have a similar format. Look at the references in published works that you are reading to get a feel for how to do it.

8.2 Referencing websites

Although the academic community was one of the first to make extensive use of the Internet and is relying increasingly on online sources in building academic knowledge, this doesn't mean that you can be any less rigorous when citing online, web-based resources. There is generally less consistency when you are citing from websites but you must remember that you still need to reference them in your writing in the normal way. That is, you need to reference the web resources you have used in the main body of the text and in the references section of your assignment. It is very important that you reference resources from the Internet in comparable ways to any other resources because downloading and copying material from the Internet without attributing the source is always regarded as plagiarism, something we discuss in more detail below. Although there are still no universal procedures for referencing web pages, there are some general conventions you need to follow in order to inform anybody reading your work where your ideas came from. You need to provide:

- the name of the website;
- the URL;
- the date the page was last updated;
- the date the website was retrieved.

Examples

Harasim, L. (2001) Shift happens: online education as a new paradigm in learning, The Internet and Higher Education, 3(1), retrieved 31 July 2002. http://virtualu.cs.sfu.ca/vuweb.newe/papers/harasim_ihe_nov00. pdf.

Law, J. (1992) Notes on the theory of actor network, Science Studies Centre, University of Lancaster, retrieved 6 August 2002. http://www.comp.lancs.ac.uk/sociology/soc054jl.html.

Do remember that you always need to include the date the web page was accessed in your reference; this way the reader can see when you found this information. Unlike published work, web addresses change, links are broken and material is removed from websites. As long as you give the URL reference as you retrieved it on a particular date, this will give the reader the opportunity to see if she can find the resource you are quoting. She can go to the homepage of the institution or organization and search for the author. She may be able to find your original reference, or it may have disappeared due to a server problem or a broken link but be visible again once the problem is rectified. It is always a good idea to check web pages again just before you finish your assignment, so that you can include the most recent access date. If you are concerned about the authority of an online resource, then you should discuss it with your tutor. You might also like to look at the section on evaluating Internet resources in Chapter 12 for more general advice. Over time you will probably find that you become better at spotting those sources which can be relied upon for their academic credibility.

8.3 Referencing other sources

With the increasing range of sources now being drawn upon by both academics and students in their writing we cannot be definitive here about how to reference every kind of source that you are likely to be referencing in your work. As we have mentioned already there are a range of online university sites available via the Internet which deal extensively with citation and referencing. It is worth spending some time exploring these and Activity Twenty-six should help you to do this.

Activity Twenty-six: Learning about citation

Search the Internet for relevant websites which give guidance on citation and referencing for university writing. Choose three different websites. On each one follow the relevant links to find out about citing 'reports'.

Compare the differences and similarities between the advice given on each different site. Now make a record of the key elements that you think should be present when citing reports and in what order they should generally appear.

When we did this task we found the key elements, which frequently appeared in this order, were:

- author(s') name(s)
- date
- title of report
- name of institution
- web page
- volume and numbering.

Now repeat the same task for the following:

- journals taken from an electronic source
- citing from lectures
- citing personal communication
- citing secondary sources
- other sources you have used/or are likely to use in an assignment which you are unsure about referencing.

Remember to keep a record of the websites you have visited when you have finished so that you can return to them again if necessary.

8.4 Recording references

It is very important that you keep a reliable record of your references as you come across them in preparation for your assignments. There are a range of bibliographic software packages available for this purpose but these tend to be quite complicated to use and probably only worth considering if you are undertaking postgraduate study. You may find it easier to record your references alphabetically and/or by course using ordinary word processing software to build up a database of references. Remember though to back it up or keep a copy on a memory stick. You can also record brief notes on why you found a particular reference useful, you can refer to important page numbers and even record complete quotes if they seem relevant to you.

8.5 Referencing and plagiarism

Before we begin to explore some of the difficulties you might encounter around using sources, citation and referencing we want to remind you of our discussions around note taking in Chapter 5. The two methods of note taking we explored there took you away from the original academic text in order to help you to develop notes and ideas that were in your own words and made sense to you. Nevertheless, we cannot stress enough that it is very important that you always make reference to the authors from whom you got the ideas in the first place. As we suggested above you will need to keep some kind of record of what you have read along with your own notes; this means that you will always be able to use your sources correctly in your writing. One of the 'rules' of academic writing is that you must always attribute ideas that 'belong' to somebody else. Put another way, you must never try to pass off as your own ideas that 'belong' to somebody else and that did not originate from you, particularly if they are published in one form or another. If you do use ideas that you know you have read in a book, article or web-based resource you must make this clear, through the use of references. If you do not then you may find yourself accused of plagiarism. If your previous experience of education has been outside an anglophone institution you may not have come across the idea of plagiarism before and, therefore, you will probably want to pay particular attention to the discussions in this chapter.

The concept of plagiarism is very complicated, not least because it is often very difficult to decide where an 'original idea' came from. If you remember, in Chapter 1 we mentioned 'talking for writing'. In seminars students and tutors talk over ideas together, ideas that may then be redigested and developed by lecturers in their own academic publications. So, in some ways, the idea of ownership of academic knowledge and ideas is very difficult to define. That said, as a student the onus is on you to make sure that you cannot be accused of plagiarism and so you must always make sure that you reference other authors' work meticulously. We discuss one particular referencing system below. If you know that you have read something in a book or found it on a website it is not worth attempting to pass the idea off as your own. It is quite likely that your tutor will know the work that you have read and know that it does not 'belong' to you. Although many students get quite worried about plagiarism, as you become a more experienced student writer you will feel more confident with what you feel are your ideas and which ones need to be referenced. It is best to start by erring on the safe side and referencing whenever you feel unsure, rather than omitting a citation. Later in this chapter we explore how you can integrate different authors and voices and use this creatively in your writing.

The easiest things to reference are direct quotes. Obviously, if you are quoting directly from a book then you must give a clear reference for it. Changing a few words around may mean that the material is no longer a direct quote, but that doesn't change the fact that it has been taken directly from a published text and needs referencing in the same way. There are two ways of using a quote from reading: allowing the quote to 'stand alone' or incorporating the gist of what the author has said more seamlessly into your own text – this is known as paraphrasing. When the quote stands alone then it is easy to put the reference immediately after it. When you are quoting in a rather general way, in a sense summarizing what the author you have read says, then you should put your reference as close as possible to your first statement or sentence about this author's ideas. Then the reader will know that the ideas that come next are likely to be a summary of somebody else's ideas that you have read, rather than ideas that you are laying claim to. This latter form of referencing can seem quite difficult and that's why you need to check with your tutor on a piece of your own written work if you are doing what is required. The following three examples from Goodman and Redclift (1991) give you an idea of the different ways in which you may see references used in published work, particularly in the social sciences. Although the examples we use here are conventional, in that they refer to books, the same principles still apply with citation to electronic resources:

1. Among the most thoughtful of these accounts, and one which places emphasis on the impact of new domestic technologies or 'white goods', is that of Bose (1982) writing about modern North American households.

2. As manufacturing took over from cottage industry, women left the domestic handloom, and their labour was transferred to the mill: 'Women had always been involved in the family production of textiles. When textile production was removed to the factories, girls entered the factory workforce. But, even in that setting, they were seen as working for the household. In Italy and France, some factory owners tried to create "family" conditions and supervision for their female employees and, on occasion, even to arrange marriages for them' (O'Day 1985: 43).The transfer of many of women's skills, and much of their labour, from the household to food processing was in some respects a similar process, occurring at a later stage in the industrialization of the United Kingdom, but there were also significant differences.

3. It was argued at the time that domestic training was not only useful in servants to the middle classes, it was also essential in working-class wives (Dawes 1984).

These examples are taken from one published work. One of the best ways of learning how to use references in your subject area is to pay attention to the ways in which the authors that you read for your studies incorporate references into their texts. In (1) direct reference is made to Bose's work on the impact of new domestic technologies. The author name is directly referenced and the date of this work is placed in brackets immediately after this. A different approach to citation is used in (2). In this case, a complete quote from O'Day's work is used and not only author name and date of publication are included but also the page number for the quote. In (3) Dawes' work is being used to support a more general statement about domestic training, a debate to which it is assumed – by the reference – that the author Dawes has made a significant contribution.

Sometimes this kind of referencing can be ambiguous and this is something you need to pay particular attention to, making sure that the meaning is as transparent as possible to the reader.

In exploring this further we consider the following example from one student's work:

4. Although real change in the conditions of production did not occur until their work was brought into factories in the process of industrialization, it could be argued that to some extent women have always been part of the labour force (O'Day 1985).

Which of these do you think best describes what the student means in making reference to O'Day's work?

a) O'Day has argued that real change did not occur until women began to work in the factories.

b) O'Day has argued that women have always been part of the labour force.

c) O'Day has argued both of the above a) and b), and the student writer is reporting this as fact.
d) O'Day has argued that real change did not occur until women's work was brought into the factories and it is the student herself who is suggesting that women have always been part of the labour force.

There is no definitively correct answer. There are a number of reasons why there may be some ambiguity about what the author O'Day said and what the student is claiming was said. For example, the student's citation to the source may have been placed too far from what it is meant to be referring to, and therefore it is unclear precisely what meaning it is meant to convey. The student may have paraphrased the source so it is difficult to establish what was said by the original author and what is the student voice.

This sentence from a student essay, which we have made up, is also ambiguous:

> Many commentators have indicated their concern with the failure of educational research to engage adequately with the ongoing problem of social disadvantage (Reddy 2005).

What do you think the writer meant when she drew on Reddy's work? What additions do you think you would like to make to this sentence to make the meaning clearer and less ambiguous?

The sentence above could mean that:

a) Reddy is one of the commentators being referred to by the student;
b) Reddy is reporting on those commentators who have indicated their concern with the failure of educational research.

We think that the meaning of this sentence would be less ambiguous if the names of the commentators were included and the reference to Reddy's work was moved forward in the sentence as follows:

> Reddy (2005) points to the fact that many commentators (see Falls 2003; Nason 2007) have indicated their concern with the failure of educational research to engage adequately with the ongoing problem of social disadvantage.

Remember that, in order to avoid ambiguity when citing sources, it is always a good idea to read your work through carefully before submitting it, paying particular attention to your use of citations and making sure they mean what you intended. (NB You will not see citation to Reddy, Falls and Nason in the references section at the end of the book because we have made these names up.)

8.6 Thinking about plagiarism

In this section we are going to explore some of the more vexing questions around plagiarism including:

- What is plagiarism?
- How might you plagiarize inadvertently?
- Are there any situations in which you do not have to cite your sources?

When you hand in your assignment the tutor will make the assumption that this is your work. This might seem self-evident and you might even be required to sign a form for verification, particularly if this piece of work is going to count towards your degree. By identifying yourself as the author you are by default laying claim to ownership of that piece of writing. If you don't identify your sources then you lay yourself open to the charge of plagiarism.

Activity Twenty-seven: Which of the following would you regard as plagiarism?

- Using a direct quote without making the source clear.
- Paraphrasing or summarizing what you have read and not indicating the citation to the original source of your ideas.
- Cutting from a source document and pasting it into your own work without making citation to the original source.
- Changing a few words around in the original source and then using it in your work without indicating where the idea came from.

As you have probably guessed all these would be regarded as plagiarism because in all cases you have attempted to pass off the authored words of others as your own. We are not interested in discussing willful plagiarism here, what some people actually call cheating. You know yourself if you are consciously trying to pass off work which is not your own in order to get a better mark than you deserve from the efforts that you personally have put into an assignment. You know if you have copied and pasted something you found on the Internet and made a few changes to the text to make it seem a bit different from the original and look like your own work. The discussion which follows is concerned with avoiding inadvertent plagiarism and how you can most effectively use the work you have read in order to support and develop a coherent argument of your own.

8.7 Using your sources creatively

In order to consider issues such as those raised in Activity Twenty-seven in more depth, in this section we are going to spend some more time thinking about how you might use your different sources in order to integrate the 'voices' of all the different authors and writers that you are drawing on when composing your own writing. As you will see from the extracts from a student essay that we examine in Activity Twenty-nine below, attributing your sources correctly is the way in which you as the assignment writer can show how your argument is being constructed through a combination of perspectives from a number of different authors, including, of course, you. By their very nature, academic ideas cannot develop without being located in a 'conversation' and using sources appropriately locates you as a student in that particular conversation. Put another way, it gives you an entry into that club as a new member. You do not come in as an expert but learn the conversation of the experts and build what you want to say around that, always making sure that you explicitly acknowledge what the experts have been saying. Avoiding plagiarism is fundamentally about making visible to the reader of your assignment the conversation you have entered into, which authors you have drawn on and where your ideas have come from. You are using sources not only to provide evidence for your argument but to construct your argument, something we have already explored in some depth in Chapter 7. The whole process of reading and assimilating what others say is central to building your argument and using appropriate referencing for all your sources helps the reader see where your ideas are coming from, what you are building on and how skilfully you are able to extend this to present your own perspective on a topic. This enables you to get credit from the assessor of your work where it is due.

Tutors often bemoan the fact that so many students submit assignments which they describe as playing safe with very little originality. Your tutor can only gauge the originality in your writing if she is able to see what you are adding to what you have read. To do this she needs to be able to understand how you have built on your sources in developing your argument in order to provide some kind of originality. This is what will earn you the best marks because it will make your work stand out from the crowd! Using sources correctly will also help you to unravel what the different authors you are using are saying, as well as helping you to synthesize these contrasting views. Looked at this way we can begin to see that using sources correctly is not just a chore but is a valuable way of working with different viewpoints. You will not only cite authors you agree with but also use authors who propose an alternative viewpoint. Through juxtaposing the views of others in this way you begin to build your own perspective on the question in hand. In short, using sources creatively is part of what it means to write at university.

Generally most subject tutors don't just want to read an essay which is full of long quotes with some linking sentences written by the student. On the other hand, it is also completely understandable that students who are concerned about plagiarism think it is best to do what tutors call 'play safe' and to quote directly from a text rather than find themselves open to accusations of plagiarism. One of the challenges you face as a student writer is finding a way to integrate the sources you are drawing on in your own work, and using them effectively to build your own argument without using too many direct quotations from the authors you are using. A helpful tool in this process of integration is to pay attention to the range of linking words you can use to make a connection in your argument between your ideas and those of the authors you are drawing from. The following activity should help you to do this.

Activity Twenty-eight: How to introduce your sources

Look at an example of one of your own assignments.

Make a list of some of the words and phrases you have used which signal the shift back and forth between your words and the words of your source author.

Now take an article you have read or one you need to read for a forthcoming assignment. Use words and phrases the author has used to add to your original list.

These are some of the ones on our list:

- discusses
- points out
- illustrates
- claims
- shows
- argues
- provides evidence
- says
- proposes
- suggests
- asserts
- assumes

In order to help you to think a little more about the integration of sources and the different 'voices' in your assignment writing we examine two similar extracts, A and B, from a student essay, below.

Activity Twenty-nine

Read Extract A.
How many writers can you identify in this text?
What is telling you who these different writers are?
Can you identify one or two examples of the 'voice' of the student who wrote this essay?

Extract A

During the 1930s and 1940s Benjamin Whorf wrote various papers concerning the connection between the structure of individual languages and their speakers' perception of reality. He suggested that the way in which humans view the world is constrained by the language available to them. In this way, measurable differences in world view could be discerned between speakers of different languages (Whorf, cited in Carroll 1956). This view of the connection between language structure and social reality is referred to as 'linguistic determinism' and has been largely discredited by linguists during the last forty years. Working primarily with the contrasting features of the language of the Hopi Indians and what he called Standard Average European languages, Whorf concluded that our perception of 'time' and 'matter' is determined by the language available to us. His work with the Hopi language suggested that there was no distinction between present, past and future and therefore its speakers could not conceptualize time in the same way as a speaker of a Standard European Language. Whorf went further than simply making a connection between language and reality to suggest that the thought processes of the individual were actually linguistically determined: 'The background linguistic system of each language is not merely a reproducing instrument for voicing ideas but rather is itself the shaper of ideas, the program and guide for the individual's mental activity' (Carroll 1956 p. 25).

Looking critically at Whorf's writings, linguists have found it difficult to verify much that he hypothesized and in some instances have been able to provide evidence that refutes his work, for example, that he was incorrect in asserting that Eskimos have many different words for snow (Pulham, source unknown, quoted by D. Hargreaves in University of Wessex seminar). Coupled with the fact that in America, in the 1950s and 1960s, Whorf's work was used in the debate which regarded black people as inferior to white and the contradictory evidence regarding 'linguistic determinism', his work became regarded by most linguists as having little validity. Taken to its logical conclusion such a hypothesis would not allow the possibility of successful translation between languages, a suggestion that is clearly absurd.

Modern linguistics has often been more concerned with identifying similarities between languages rather than differences, particularly influenced by work on language universals (Chomsky 1965). Although there may be little place for 'linguistic determinism' in modern day linguistics, since Whorf was writing there has been both continued and renewed interest in the issue of 'linguistic relativity'. How far can language be said to shape world view and what are the connections between language and the culture in which the language is spoken? 'Linguistic relativity' is a much weaker version of the determinist position suggesting a connection between an individual's language and their own perception of reality but not suggesting the severity of constraints on reality that a purely determinist position would imply. Within this relativist position the individual is seen as having a perception of the world which is in some way limited by the language available to her. On the other hand, implicit in this position is that she can use this language to construct other interpretations of the world. There is no suggestion that the language system is so fixed that only one world view is possible. The principle of 'linguistic relativity' seems to be most useful for linguists in consideration of the ways in which culture is mediated through language. Rather than looking at contrast between languages, as Whorf did, the modern linguist often appears more concerned with language use within one culture, or one nation state, where speakers are identified as generally speaking the same language.

Language cannot be viewed in isolation from the culture in which it is spoken. As Hymes (1974) identified, what is important is the communicative event, the circumstances in which language use takes place, who says what to whom and how meanings are interpreted by the participants within any communicative event. Linguists have long made the distinction between the language system and language use in the tradition of Saussure's (cited in Cameron 1985) dichotomy between 'langue' and 'parole'. Chomsky (1965) distinguishes language 'competence' from language 'performance'. From a theoretical perspective linguists have looked closely at what may constitute a system of language, identifying elements of language in a grammatical framework that could be regarded as language universals. At the same time, sociolinguists have concentrated on language use rather than system, seeing system as a purely theoretical construct since language cannot be identified outside the circumstances in which it is being used.

Discussion

In relation to Activity Twenty-nine (above) we have identified nine obvious writers in this extract, including all those authors cited as primary, secondary or personal sources: Whorf, Carroll, Pulham, Hargreaves, Chomsky, Hymes, Saussure, Cameron and the student writer herself. We were able to recognize the authors the student had drawn on because she made appropriate reference, either directly to their work, to the work of another author who had cited the original work, e.g. 'Whorf, cited in Carroll 1956', or to a personal source, e.g. Pulham, source unknown, quoted by D. Hargreaves in University of Wessex seminar.

We thought that this sentence was clearly the voice of the student:

> Taken to its logical conclusion such a hypothesis would not allow the possibility of successful translation between languages, a suggestion that is clearly absurd.

Activity Thirty

Now read Extract B.

Extract B

During the 1930s and 1940s Benjamin Whorf wrote various papers about the connection between the structure of individual languages and their speakers' perception of reality. He suggested that the way in which humans view the world is constrained by the language available to them. In this way measurable differences in world view could be discerned between speakers of different languages. This view of the connection between language structure and social reality is called 'linguistic determinism' and has been largely discredited by linguists during the last forty years. Taking, for example, the perception of 'time' in different cultures; it might seem something different to people who speak different languages and come from different cultures. For example, if people from different cultures have different ways of talking about the concepts of present, past and future, it might mean that speakers from different cultures don't necessarily all understand 'time' in the same way. Looked at in this way, it is possible to argue that this is more than simply making a connection between language and reality. That is language does not merely reflect the world as it is but actually constructs it in particular ways depending on the cultural context. So, for example, Eskimos have lots of words for snow because they live in a world where making these distinctions is crucial to their day to day life. However you look at it we can see that language shapes ideas and guides mental activity but some linguists have provided evidence that this is just a myth. Also, in America, in the 1950s and 1960s, Whorf's work was used in the debate which regarded black people as inferior to white, and because of this and the contradictory evidence regarding 'linguistic determinism' his work became regarded by most linguists as having little validity. Taken to its logical conclusion such a hypothesis would not allow the possibility of successful translation between languages, a suggestion that is clearly absurd.

Maybe what is more important are the similarities between languages rather than the differences. This is what Chomsky was interested in when he described things that were universally found in all languages. But modern linguists are more interested in 'linguistic relativity' (http://en.wikipedia.org/wiki/Principle_of_linguistic_relativity) and issues about how far language can be said to shape world view and what are the connections between language and the culture in which the language is spoken. This is a much weaker version of the determinist position. Within a relativist position the individual is seen as having a perception of the world which is in some way limited by the language available to her. On the other hand, implicit in this position is that she can use this language to construct other interpretations of the world. There is no suggestion that the language system is so fixed that only one world view is possible. The principle of 'linguistic relativity' seems to be most useful for linguists in consideration of the ways in which culture is mediated through language. Rather than looking at the contrast between languages we should be more interested in looking at the way people use language within one culture, or one nation where everyone is speaking the same language.

If you try to ask yourself the same questions as you did for Extract A (see Activity Twenty-nine), you will probably find them a lot more difficult to answer. The lack of citations in Extract B means that it is difficult to establish where the student is drawing from a source such as a published work. It appears that there is just one voice, that of the student, but in reality the writer has drawn her understanding of the debates from other authors. However, the only specific citation is with respect to her use of the term 'linguistic relativity', where she has cited a web page from wikipedia. Although this can be a quick and easy way of finding out where else to look for other sources about a topic, it is not usually regarded as a reliable source – in itself – for discussion of specific academic concepts and terms. This is because anybody can edit entries on this and other similar wiki sites, which means that it is neither reliable nor authoritative in the same way as more established academic publications and web-based resources.

In contrast to the use of sources in Extract A, with Extract B it would be very difficult for the tutor who marked this work to know what the student had actually read and how she had drawn upon this in developing her own argument in her assignment. In other words, we cannot see which writers – or whose work – have contributed to this text. Although it does begin with some general reference to the author, Whorf, it is difficult for the reader to establish what are the students' ideas and her interpretation of Whorf's work and/or what perspectives she has developed from what she has read which has been written by other authors. As she makes so little use of citations she appears to be claiming the ideas she is writing about. We cannot be sure of her intentions and whether this is a deliberate intention to plagiarize; it may just be due to poor record keeping on her part or she may be genuinely rushed and have no record of either what she read or where she has noted things down verbatim from another author. Nevertheless, from the tutor's point of view, if it is obvious that the student is paraphrasing the words of others without appropriate citation, then this will be regarded as plagiarism. This is one reason why we encourage you to be rigorous about your note taking in terms of the resources you have used.

We hope that by the time you have read and worked through the activities in this chapter you will agree that avoiding plagiarism is not just a chore but at the very heart of developing your own argument. Whilst, on the one hand, it is about putting you and your voice into the heart of your writing, it is also about being a member of an academic community with its own conventions and ways of writing. As we have indicated already these conventions vary between subjects and disciplines and your tutor is always the best person to ask for advice about citation conventions in your particular subject, course or module.

Notes

- It is always best to 'err on the safe side' when it comes to referencing.
- Even when using the Internet as a resource you must still reference meticulously.
- Check your own subject-based sources to find out how to cite different kinds of publications.
- Avoiding plagiarism is not just a chore but a way of working creatively with your sources.

9

Putting yourself into your academic writing

One student's dilemma • 'Parrot writing' • Can you be 'original' in your university writing? • Using 'I' in your assignments • From the personal to the academic

Is the tutor interested in my ideas?

Do I have to simply leave myself out of my university writing?

I came to university to explore my own ideas – but are they interested in what I think?

Can I use 'I' in my university writing?

In this chapter we take up work on the topic of the family begun in Chapter 2, to look again at the relationship between your own identity as a writer and the academic writing you do at university. In Chapter 1 and elsewhere we have suggested ways to help you to develop fluency and confidence in the process of writing and to think of yourself as a writer. We have talked about the importance of using your own words to help you to bridge the gap that may seem to exist between ways in which you have been used to thinking about the world and those you encounter in different fields of study and disciplines. We have explored how you can get into the kinds of writing that are appropriate for university, looking at ways of moving from descriptive to analytic writing and of developing an argument. Now we move on to think about the rather complex question of how you can get yourself, your own 'voice', into your assignment. Do you have a feeling of ownership about your university writing or are you floundering around trying to *behave* like a university student writer? What does 'putting yourself into an assignment' mean? Students are often concerned by their sense of the gap between what they are interested in and want to say, and the requirements of university writing that, in many subject areas, seem to expect students not to involve themselves personally at all. We will consider this issue in university writing with the following questions in mind:

- What is your relationship to your own writing? Can you have a sense of yourself in your writing even when you are trying to keep to the conventions of the subject you are studying?
- Can you bring your own ideas, opinions and sense of identity into university writing? How far will this show in your use of the first person in your work?

9.1 One student's dilemma

On the matter of getting himself into his assignment one student said this:

> I try to stick as much to references as possible. I have to have the relevant data . . . In the actual essay I don't interject myself . . . I just go with everything that somebody can actually go back and check . . . because I'm not an authority. In other words, whenever I write something there must be an authority . . . The problem is when you are writing there is always a tendency to forget the academic side of it and you go and put in anecdotes and whatever and you think 'good' and you think everything is flowing. So sometimes you think you'll have a go but you know that is wrong and you have to cut it out.

This student's dilemma about his sense that he has to leave out his own ideas for his assessed work because he is 'not an authority', coupled with his satisfaction that his work is 'flowing' when he can 'forget the academic side', illustrates a common problem for students. His difficulty is that he has not yet found a way of bringing his own good work into what he sees as the university requirements. He does not think he is 'good enough' – his work must be 'wrong'. For this reason he is not really giving himself the chance to use what he knows and can do already in his writing.

We will suggest that there are ways in which you may be 'present' in a piece of writing even when it is apparently 'impersonal'. One theme of this chapter is the importance of your personal engagement with what you are studying, so that through your writing you come to have a sense of ownership of what you have produced. As you write assignments you have the opportunity to make the ideas you are engaging with a part of your own thinking and understanding so that each time you complete an assignment, hand it in and hopefully get feedback on it, it is possible to think of it as your own production. This is why we have stressed the importance of using your own words to understand your university assignments and reading. This sense of ownership is important if you are to get satisfaction from your university writing, as well as for learning the subject. The very process of engaging with ideas through writing about them helps to make them a part of your identity as a writer and, in this way, your commitment to the task of writing can result in a much stronger piece of work. This kind of commitment to learning a subject is illustrated in the following students' comments:

> I wanted to understand how our political system works.

> I need to know about accounting because I want to run a small business.

> I cry sometimes when I see a movie and I want to try to understand why.

> I need to teach my pupils to read, and need all the understanding that I can get.

Similarly, a university tutor and researcher wrote this about his reasons for doing research and his experience of writing:

> The reason I undertake research undoubtedly reinforces my difficulties in writing. For I generally choose subjects because I simultaneously feel that they are important and I am uncertain about my own views on them. I research the subject in the attempt to clarify my own conclusions on them.
>
> (*ExChanges* 1996)

9.2 'Parrot writing'

We explored in Chapter 5 how, as you find out more about your assignment topic from more sources, you always need to be processing for yourself the material you use, formulating and putting together your ideas in writing, and incorporating them into your own thinking. You need to negotiate and work with the demands of university writing, not just try to adopt them wholesale; this produces 'imitation' writing, which is neither convincing to the tutor nor in the long run satisfying to you, the student. As the English tutor quoted in Chapter 3 said, students begin to 'parrot these discourses' before they have really got inside them. This may not always be a bad way to begin to get hold of the subject, for imitating a writer you are reading can be a good way of getting the feel of what he or she is saying. It is certainly also useful to look closely at how writers write. However, in general, just trying to use a particular style or vocabulary is to try to imitate the surface features of a discipline, without really getting into its way of thinking, and in the end it does not work. Students who do this end up with strange and confused pieces of writing, rather like children trying to use unfamiliar, adult language. They do not feel confident and do not enjoy writing. We might compare this with playing a piece of music without understanding anything about rhythm. Individual notes may be right but they don't fit together into a recognizable piece of music. In the end, therefore, we are saying that you have to develop your own way of writing a subject, however modestly, and the activities we have provided in this book often ask you to start to get into university reading or writing by using your own words. Slowly your own way becomes related to your new role as a university student and you get a sense of yourself as the writer of your university assignments. You become confident that you are able to handle university writing, even though you will not always get it right at first; but then, neither do academics, who also have to struggle every time they write something new.

In the following activity about your relationship to your assignment, you need to write out your answers in your own, exploratory way. Such writing may serve as a personal record of your thinking, helping you progressively to clarify your thinking as you work. We will ask you to return to this activity at the end of the chapter.

Activity Thirty-one: Thinking about your place in an assignment

Choose an assignment title that you may have to write, and think about the questions below:

- What is your interest in the subject?
- Will you be able to include your own opinions and experiences in the assignment?
- What kinds of satisfaction might you get from completing this assignment?
- Will you expect to use 'I' in the assignment? Think about your reasons for this answer.

Commentary

Here are some examples of the kinds of satisfactions students report that they get from writing:

I enjoyed the reading, really finding out more about the subject.

It was hard but it was very satisfying to see a whole essay that I'd done, ready to hand in.

> I liked having to sort out my ideas and I really felt I knew the subject when I'd finished.
>
> I'd always been interested in politics and now I felt I was understanding how it all works.

9.3 Can you be 'original' in your university writing?

University teachers sometimes seem to be asking for two contradictory things in their students' assignments. They say that they want to know what you are thinking, and, at the same time, insist that you make use of what academic writers have said. What they really mean is: first you have to get into our way of looking at things and then you can begin to say it in your own way. This is not such a contradiction as it sounds, because, of course, all our ideas have 'come' from somewhere else. At university much of your 'experience' and knowledge come from reading what other people have said. As we have stressed in previous chapters, what is important is that you are able to make your own use of your sources when you re-form them for your own purposes for writing. So, although it is true that when you write for university you have to draw on what others have said, this does not necessarily mean that you have to give up your own ideas, but you do have to clarify what you think and present this in a way that does not solely depend on your own personal experience. Personal and individual viewpoints may well be relevant but they have to be set in a context. This may mean that you have to distance yourself from your personal perspective and see it in a wider framework. We have explored how there can be very different ways of examining topics from different subject and discipline perspectives, and you have to make sure that you can take account of this when you are writing different assignments, often for different tutors. In the end, it may be true that writing for university can mean that there is a contradiction between your wish to have your say and the requirements of the subject you are writing. If you really want to write directly about your own experiences and ideas, you may have to do it in other ways. Experienced writers write in different ways at different times. On the other hand, it can be possible to find ways of relating the 'personal' and the 'academic'. Sometimes students come to study a particular subject precisely because they want to get a new perspective on what they have experienced, and such study can be very satisfying for them. As we explore in the readings below, there are various ways of writing yourself into your academic assignment.

9.4 Using 'I' in your assignments

Students are often puzzled as to whether they can use the first person in their university assignments. The tutors quoted in Chapter 3 indicate the range of views about this. The question is closely related to the larger question of your relationship to your material, and your sense of your identity as the writer of the assignment. There may be a wide range of reasons for the use of the first person in a piece of writing. For example, you might want to signal that the ideas you are presenting are not definitive. It might be that you want to write about your personal opinion at some points and you want to separate this from some other parts of the assignment where you do not use 'I'. Often writers use 'I' in their introduction to establish their place in relation to their material, and then go on to present the material itself in a more distanced fashion. Above all, the use of 'I' can establish a sense of a relation between writer and reader and between the writer and their material. In the following activity we ask you to investigate writers' use – or non-use – of the first person by looking at some course materials.

Activity Thirty-two: The use of 'I' in course materials

Check some of the books or course materials you have to hand to see whether they use 'I', and, if so, where they use it and what the reason might be. Think about what effect the use or non-use of 'I' has on the relationship between reader and writer.

The matter of using the first person in your assignments is difficult to address because conventions vary between subjects. In fact, in some subjects the use of 'I' is encouraged and in others it is actually 'forbidden'. This can also vary between tutors, even within a single subject area. In some cases, the subject or the tutor is flexible about it and you may well find that it is quite acceptable to make use of the first person as long as you know why you are doing it. The use of the first person is also related to the question of bringing your own opinion into your work. In some subjects tutors will say that they want to know what you think, while in other subjects your own thinking is viewed as irrelevant. This kind of difference can be very frustrating for students. What are you meant to do?

You may have begun a course because it seemed to be about your own interests, but then you find that you are not expected to bring in your own experiences or opinions or yourself after all. You may find that you are expected to write as if you were not present in a situation when you were. For example, if you have carried out a science experiment, you will probably be expected to use the passive tense: to say 'this was done' and not 'I did this'. In social studies you may carry out an interview and yet not reveal this when you write about it. You may have been moved by a film but are rarely expected to discuss your feelings about it in a film studies assignment.

Underlying these questions is your position in relation to your material. Most importantly, if you do use 'I' and bring your own opinions into your university writing, you are still meant to stand outside your material and to be able to be objective about it, to think about it without being emotional or one-sided in your opinions. This distance from the subject matter is a mark of academic writing, even when it is clear that the writer has a strong view about their subject. Yet it is still possible for you to have a sense of ownership of your material and authority in your writing if you are confident about using the subject matter. However, it can be difficult to get enough confidence to think that what you write will be adequate when you are dealing with a new subject. It is therefore equally difficult to claim the 'right' to write as 'I' when you don't yet have a clear sense of your identity as a writer of that subject.

What is it like to write as 'I'? It is important to remember that whenever we use 'I' in writing, the 'I' character is in a sense a fictional construction created for the purpose of claiming the right to say something in this particular piece. Just as we talk differently to different people in different situations, in writing our sense of 'I' depends on whom we are addressing and why, and how we are writing. Your university 'I' is different in each assignment you write.

In general, if you are not told otherwise, our advice is to use 'I' if it seems sensible for your purposes. Don't pretend that you don't exist in your assignment if you do, even if you have to find ways of putting yourself there such as, 'It seems to me . . .' or, more impersonally, 'The evidence seems to suggest . . .'. This is a good example of the writer who is 'there' in her writing, since it is she who is drawing the conclusion, while claiming that the conclusion just comes from 'the evidence'. However, she is only present in the writing invisibly, which is often the case in academic writing. She does not use 'I' because she seems to be suggesting that the 'evidence' is more important than her own views. We will explore this apparent 'disappearance' of the writer further in the readings below.

9.5 From the personal to the academic

One way of thinking about the specificity of academic writing is to compare it with what we can broadly term 'personal' writing, where the writer is obviously at its centre and there seems to be a clear relationship between what is written and the writer. Then you can think of writing for university as a shift from a personal to an academic way of thinking and writing, involving shifts in the writer's sense of 'I' in their writing in specific ways. The following activity is linked to the work you did on the differences between an auto-biographical and an academic text in Activity Eleven, but the focus is different: here we are asking you to consider things from the perspective of yourself, the writer, rather than yourself the reader, and, in particular, to think about your identity and position within your own different kinds of writing.

Activity Thirty-three: Writing from a personal perspective

Identify an event in your childhood that was important to you. When you have decided on this, write one or two paragraphs about it, indicating what happened and how it was important. Imagine that you are writing for a friendly fellow student or tutor. Note that we are asking you to write briefly on a subject that could be a lengthy piece of work tackled in many different ways. If you can, carry out this activity with another student and discuss each other's writing.

When you have finished, read over what you have written and note how often you have used 'I'. Can you say from this piece what the 'I' character is like and what he or she seems to be doing in the account?

Does the 'I' character seem to identify with the child or an adult looking on at the child?

Can you identify features of the writing that show that it is 'personal'?

Compare what you note with the table below and keep this piece of writing in mind as you look at the readings below.

The following table sets out some of the major differences we suggest that you might find between 'personal' and 'academic' writing. Keep this in mind as you work on the activity related to the passages below.

Personal writing	Academic writing
Recounts, tells a personal story	Comments, evaluates, analyses
Non-technical vocabulary	Subject-specific vocabulary
'I' at the centre of the story	'I' as the observer and commentator
Information comes from the writer's experience	Information comes from a range of sources, and refers to what others say
Personal feelings and views	Evidence and argument
	Conventions of referencing and citing to acknowledge others' work

We now move on to illustrate what we have been saying about the writer's place in their writing. In the following activity and commentary we ask you to think about three different extracts from readings. We have chosen these particular passages because they show how there are both differences and similarities between what we are calling 'personal' and 'academic' writing, and in order to give you an idea of ways in which you can move between these different kinds of writing. We will suggest that there is more of a continuum than a complete break between personal and academic writing and that there are various different ways for you to 'own' your university writing. The three passages below are all related to the topic of the family and are all written by women. The first is a 'personal' piece of writing which recounts an event in the writer's childhood, while the other two are different kinds of academic writing.

Activity Thirty-four: The writer's place in personal and academic writing

Read the following three passages and check them against the list of 'personal' and 'academic' features in the table above. Answer the questions below about each of them.

- Does the passage tell us anything about the writer?
- Where does the information come from?
- Does the writer present any of her own opinions?
- How does she do this?

Remember that we are asking you to think about these passages in order to think about what you are doing when you write yourself.

Passage 1
When I was 9 years old my parents split up and I went to live with my mother and new stepfather. My brother stayed at home with my father. This split-up of the family was very painful to me at the time because it was as though I had lost my father and my brother and our family home all at once. I think it made me less confident than I had been.

(Carol, a postgraduate student)

Passage 2
However, it should also be clear that it is not easy for women to survive as heads of single-parent families. Female-headed households face a situation of relative social isolation. Especially in the early stages of the domestic cycle, single-parent women must both work for money and do all the domestic chores. This leaves no time to establish and extend relationships. Indeed, it is often difficult for them to maintain relationships with kin. There is the money problem too. Female-headed households, since they are very poor, do not have material resources to get involved in social exchange. Esperanza's case is illustrative of this point.

(González de la Rocha 1994: 211)

Passage 3

Briefly, the family politics were as follows: Elizabeth Barrett was the eldest of eleven children living with her parents at 'Hope End' in Ledbury, Herefordshire. As a small child her precocious talent was recognized and rewarded by her father. In her diary she wrote: 'In my sixth year for some lines on virtue which I had penned with great care I received from Papa a ten shilling note enclosed in a letter which was addressed to the Poet Laureat [sic] of Hope End'. Encouraged by paternal approval she continued to turn out masses of apprentice stuff, generally rehashes of works by male authors, such as her 'Battle of Marathon' in imitation of Pope. Of all her siblings, she was closest to her brother Edward, nicknamed Bro', born in 1807, one year after Elizabeth. They all spent their time together – climbing, fishing, horseriding, organizing plays and picnics. She shared Bro's tutor, Mr McSwiney, and learned Greek with him. But when Bro' left for Charterhouse Mr McSwiney left too. On the last page of the diary there is a striking sense of an ungendered Paradise Lost: 'My past days now appear as a bright star glimmering far, faraway and I feel almost agony to turn from it for ever!' She plotted that when she was grown-up she would 'wear men's clothes and live on a Greek island, the sea melting into turquoise all around it'.

The day Bro' left for school at the age of 13, Elizabeth realized that there was an inescapable difference between being a clever boy and being a clever girl. She was literally 'left behind' at what now seemed the aptly named 'Hope End'. Figuratively she was afraid of being left behind intellectually and was consumed with envy of the previously beloved brother.

(Hirsch 1995: 120)

Commentary on Passage 1

Passage 1 appears to be a 'personal' piece because it refers to the writer's own experience as a child and is written as a narrative – it recounts what happened to her and describes the effects on herself as a child, in the way that you might have done in the previous activity. The writer's place is indicated in her use of 'I'. However, note that the use of 'I' might not tell us as much about the writer as we might think. It could stand for a fictional character, invented by the writer. Alternatively, the writer could have written about her own experience by using 'she', the third person. This indicates how the meaning of the use of 'I' is not a simple one, but rather it is always a construct. This passage is just about this writer's experience and her own feelings and thoughts about it. She does not make any attempt to see the events from the viewpoint of anyone else, even her parents or brother, and she does not draw on any other sources for her information. The writer is at the centre of this passage and her concern is with her own experience and feelings. She does not try to be objective and she does not draw on any 'evidence', even from her own experience, to back up her assessment that 'I think it made me less confident'. She does not need to, since she is only talking about her own experience for her own purpose. In this brief extract, she simply allows this statement to stand. The vocabulary is simple and direct, with no technical terms.

You will see, however, that, as well as recounting what happened, the writer does also make an attempt to evaluate the effects of the event on herself: 'I think it made me less confident'. Look out for this pattern, which is very common in academic writing, where a section of chronology writing, recounting what happened, or description writing is followed by a commentary. Writing as an adult about her childhood means that the writer has become a little distanced from her experience and can be a little more objective about it, which is what academic writing asks of you.

Is there any way in which this writer's experience might be useful if she were writing an assignment about the impact of parental separation on the children? Could it help her to make a statement such as the following?

> I will argue that parental separation may lead to a loss of confidence in the child.

Even if she were able to write about herself in a university assignment (and this is possible, although it would not be usual), it is clear that this writer's own experience cannot justify the above assertion. She has not explained how she became less confident or discussed other ways in which the experience affected her. In this brief passage she has not analysed her statement, even for herself. If asked to explain further, she might try to 'give evidence' that would demonstrate how she became less confident, or to think about other ways in which the experience affected her. This might lead her to think more about her experience in ways that could help her to understand it further. However, as it stands, there is nothing in her story that could allow her to generalize from her story. She cannot deduce or generalize anything about the effects of parental separation on children just from her own experience. At the same time, however, it is possible that if this writer were to make a study of the family, for instance for a social studies course, she would bring her own experience to bear on her work and it would make her study a richer experience for her. Students often say that academic study illuminates and expands their previous understanding and helps them to make sense of things in their lives or in the world around them. Writing helps reinforce this kind of learning.

How, then, might Carol approach this academic essay about the effects on the child of parental separation? To reach a more objective and academic perspective she would have to find out about what other writers have said, which she could use as her secondary sources. If this were appropriate for her particular assignment, it might also be useful to talk to other people about their experience, but she would need to acknowledge how she had got this information. She might need to engage in some kind of field research to get information at first hand, although this would be more likely to take place at a later stage in a course. Carol's own experience as a child could be a motivator for tackling such an essay, as a way of relating her own experience to that of other people and of making more sense of it, but she would now have to think about the family in different ways. She might have to rethink what a family is in terms of the perspective of her field of study. As she gathered more information she might possibly rethink what she had experienced as a child. It is unlikely that this experience would get into her writing directly, although she might be so convinced about the validity of her personal experience and opinion about her family's split-up that she would look for studies to back it up and in doing this she would discover a range of different positions, opinions and frameworks. In all this work her own experience might give her more of a sense of engagement with the work of the assignment. However, in most conventional academic writing the reader would never know about the writer's personal situation, although there might be an opportunity to bring it up – and hear from others – in seminars or other group discussions.

In this academic work the writer might or might not use 'I'. But if she does, the 'I' will be a different character from the one who is telling the reader about her childhood story. It might, for example, introduce the assignment – 'In this essay I will . . .' or 'I interviewed . . .' – or evaluate material – 'It seems to me that these two studies contradict each other'. In this case, the 'I' character would represent the writer as university student writer, distanced from her material and reasonably objective.

Commentary on Passage 2

In Passage 2 there is no use of 'I' and the passage does not refer to the writer herself. In academic fashion she has been written out of it. The question of single-parent families is treated as a social and economic issue rather than as an individual matter, so that 'the family' is placed in a wider context. The title of the book, *The Resources of Poverty: Women and Survival in the Mexican City*, tells us that the discussion is about 'poverty in Mexico', which we would not know from the extract. The information about single-parent families in this extract sounds authoritative, and makes categorical generalizations about the economic situation of 'female-headed families'. We would expect to find out about the sources for this information in the book's references section, as the use of a comprehensive referencing system and the use of other writers for information and ideas is one mark of academic writing. (You will remember that we discussed referencing in Chapter 8.) When you are writing academically you can never just rely on your own experience and ideas, you always have to refer to what others have said in the same subject area and on the same topic. The vocabulary is quite simple in this example but the terms 'female-headed households', 'kin' and 'domestic cycle' belong to the vocabulary of the social sciences (in this case social anthropology) and would seem oddly out of place in Passage 1.

Although we would not know it from this passage, you may not be surprised to learn, and you would know if you had the whole book in your hand, that the writer is, in fact, herself a woman. The use of an individual case study (which sounds as if it is a study the writer has made herself) brings in a more personal dimension to the writing, and this brings both the material and the sense of the writer's presence nearer to the reader. It is likely that the reader will respond to a sense that the writer has an interest in telling us about the difficult conditions of the women. However, this is not actually stated in the text, with its impersonal approach. Such information is often, however, given in the preface or introduction of a book.

An important feature of academic writing is that it often moves back and forth from generalizations to particular examples that support the generalization. In this passage this move is made by the mention of the case study, which, we are told, will illustrate the general point made in the first part of the paragraph. For this reason, the 'story', or case study, of 'Esperanza' will be treated not so much as an interesting story in its own right as an illustration and example of how single mothers are able to cope with their economic and socially isolated position.

Commentary on Passage 3

In Passage 3 also there is no use of 'I', and again we seem to know nothing about the writer as a person. We might have to turn to the title page of the book to find out that she is a woman. However, the passage is written from a feminist perspective; for example, it uses the term 'sexual politics' in the first section and the whole passage is about the sexual politics of the family. Although there is no 'I' character or even a sense of an individual writing, we are presented with a strongly expressed perspective on the family as a place of 'struggle' for Elizabeth Barrett. We might assume that because it is a feminist text this means that the writer is a woman, which is in fact true, but of course it need not be the case. But a particular point of view obviously comes from somewhere – and someone. Interestingly, there are two 'writer characters' in this passage – the author character, who is not expressed as 'I', and Elizabeth, who appears as the 'I' writer of her diary, where she conveys her experiences and feelings strongly: 'My past days now appear as a bright star glimmering far, faraway and I feel almost agony to turn from it for ever!' In this diary there is not even a sense of commentary and distance from her own experience as there was in Passage 1. However, the writer of the passage creates this distance from Elizabeth's experience by her selection from and commentary on it. Like much academic writing, she is writing about what another writer said. Although Elizabeth's story is presented as interesting in its own right, it is mainly used as an 'example' of how family sexual politics works, rather like the case study in Passage 2.

This writer comments on Elizabeth's feelings, and does not say what her own are. Yet her use of Elizabeth's very personal diaries does invite the reader's sympathy. Her language also seems to be coloured by that of Elizabeth's strong feelings. Compare the writer's 'she . . . was consumed with envy of her previously beloved brother' with Elizabeth's 'I feel almost agony to turn away from it for ever!' This writer has made it clear that she has taken up a position in her thinking about Elizabeth as an example of how women have been at a disadvantage in education and self-expression. She does not appear in the passage directly but she is clearly there as a slightly ghostly presence, with strongly held views.

Passages 2 and 3, then, are examples of how the writer seems to have found a place in her writing even when she does not appear directly in it. In other kinds of writing the writer seems to be more distanced from her material – for example, in an account of a scientific experiment or a report. Here are two examples, but remember that even these conceal the writer:

> The present study was undertaken to determine how *C. albicans* contributes to this lethal shock synergism . . . Because *C. albicans* and endotoxin share a number of characteristics . . . candidal infected mice were examined for induced TNF.
>
> (Berkenkotter and Huckin 1995: 55)

> In the state sector there was no difference in average A-level points score at single-sex and co-educational comprehensives, but the familiar pattern did show up among the grammars. The few remaining grammar schools had by far and away the best performance of state schools and that is where single-sex education is still mainly to be found. Of the 310 single-sex state schools, 35.5 per cent are grammar; of the 1600 co-educational schools, only 2.3 per cent are.
>
> (Smithers and Robinson 1995: 4)

In summary, then, in academic forms of writing it is unusual for the writer to appear directly and, even when she uses the first person, to appear merely as an observer and commentator, impersonally and at a distance from her material. This may be what it looks like to an outsider. However, as we have explored, you yourself as a writer may know better. You know why you may have chosen to write about a particular topic, what your interest is in it and how much of yourself you have put into it, even when you are writing about what other writers have said. The following activity asks you to think again about your place in your assignment.

Activity Thirty-five: Your place in an assignment

Think back to the assignment you chose to think about in Activity Thirty-one. Have you anything to add about your relationship to the assignment, about your use of 'I' and the use of your own thinking?

Think again: Why did you choose this assignment?

In this chapter we have been saying that you get a sense of ownership of your academic assignment by engaging with it, by your motivation for studying a subject, your choice of topic and material, and your work in organizing your ideas into an argument that you yourself put together. As you get more experience in your university work you will find that you are able to write with more authority about your subject and you will feel that there is more of yourself in what you write, however objective it is and however impersonal it looks to the reader. You yourself are becoming the writer of each assignment you produce.

Notes

- Take into account your own ideas, knowledge and experience when you are planning an assignment, but don't expect to use them 'neat' – build on them and stand back from them. Relate them to what you learn from other sources.
- Use 'I' in an academic way if you think it is appropriate.
- Don't use 'I' just to tell your own story but think about your 'university I' as an observer and commentator.
- If you are concerned, check with your tutor about the use of 'I' on their course.
- Remember that university writing never just tells a story (recounts what happened), although this may often be an element in an assignment.
- Take note of how writers establish or suggest what their position is in relation to their material. Don't expect this last point to be always obvious. You may have to search a bit.

10

Putting it together

Writing the introduction • Writing the conclusion • Reviewing your work: redrafting and editing • Editing for the reader • Reviewing your work: what are you looking for? • Reorganizing your work: an example

What am I supposed to do about the introduction and conclusion?

I don't need to know what you are going to say.

Do tell your reader what you are going to say.

I never really read my work through.

In this chapter we come to the final stages of preparing your assignment, when you have it nearly complete but not quite ready: the stage when you need to make sure that it will be well presented. We do want to emphasize that this is a very important and also a time-consuming stage in writing an assignment. Students who are not very used to writing course assignments sometimes find this surprising. It is easy to assume that by the time the whole assignment is written, often after considerable effort, the only thing left is to hand it in to the tutor with a sigh of relief. This is a mistake! Tutors are quite shocked to find out that sometimes their students haven't read over their work before handing it in. Once the piece of writing is complete you do need to review it as a whole to make sure that it is as good as you can make it. This might need to be done more than once for different purposes – for example, for checking if it 'fits together', for changing the wording or the order, for cutting redundant or repetitive parts, or for eliminating small errors. Before this, we need to consider the introduction and the conclusion.

10.1 Writing the introduction

In university writing you will be expected to provide some kind of introduction to your assignment. It may seem strange to tackle the introduction at
such a late stage. The reason for including it here is that in practice you can
only finalize the introduction once you have written the whole assignment
and, except for a final review, have got it into a shape that you find acceptable.
This will be obvious if you accept that you may not know what you think until
you have written it down. It is only when you have completed a piece of
writing that you can introduce it to the reader.

This said, however, some writers find that writing the introduction first gives
them a sense of assurance about where they are going. It can help them to feel
grounded with a good sense of direction – it serves as a map. However, if you
decide to use the introduction in this way you definitely need to return to it to
check if it still really works in this way, because one of the points of the introduction is that it is written particularly with the reader in mind. It is also
necessary to check that you introduce what you have actually written rather
than what you thought you were writing. So our advice is that if you do feel
the need for the security of writing your introduction first to get you going, do
this quite quickly. Don't spend a long time getting it 'right' – because it may
turn out not to be right after all when you have finished the whole assignment.
It is only too easy for students to get bogged down in trying to write the
introduction and to spend too much time struggling with a task that would be
much easier if it were left until later.

Advice on university writing always stresses the importance of the introduction, and sometimes the introduction is prescribed quite specifically. For
example, the following is a common formula:

- Introduction: Tell the reader what you are going to do in the essay.
- Main body: Present your argument.
- Conclusion: Say how you have done what you promised in the introduction
  and bring everything together.

However, as we illustrated in Chapter 3, this formula only applies in some
cases. In practice, there are many different ways of introducing and concluding
a piece of work, depending on the subject, the task and the length of your
assignment. On the whole, the longer the work, the longer the introduction.

You will probably find that you get different kinds of advice about the introduction from tutors in different subject areas. As always, you will need to find
out what these are. For example, one tutor may say that you should announce
what you are going to say in an essay with 'a good clear introduction', while a
tutor in another subject says that this would be redundant and rather boring
information: 'I don't need to be told what you are going to say; I'll find out

soon enough'. Therefore, although the reader does need to know where the essay will take them, the exact form of the introduction will vary according to the particular conventions of the subject as well as any particular requirements of an individual assignment.

Although it is difficult to lay down rules as to what exactly the introduction should look like, you will be able to work out what is needed in your own way if you bear in mind that the major function of an introduction is to provide the reader with a clear signpost to where the whole piece is going. Then you will realize that there are different ways of doing this, and that the introduction, of course, depends on the piece of writing it introduces.

What the introduction may do

- Give an overview of what the piece will be about.
- Present the central idea of the assignment.
- Give reasons for writing this piece.
- Explain how the title will be interpreted.
- Give reasons for answering a question in a particular way.
- Introduce the questions the essay will be addressing.
- Give the background to the main topic of the essay; the history and/or the context.
- Make a bold statement that the rest of the essay will fill out and justify.
- Quote from somewhere else in order to interest the reader and give a feel for what the whole essay is about.
- Present a concrete example or story which the piece will explain or elaborate upon.
- Relate the assignment to other work in the same field.
- Convey the writer's own relationship both to the material of the assignment and to the reader, and a sense of their own voice in the assignment.

Activity Thirty-six: Investigating introductions

Look at the introduction to two articles in your subject area. Where does each introduction end? What work is it doing? Which of the functions in the above list apply to them? Now compare what you think with the following examples.

Below are examples of parts of four introductions – in most cases, the first sentence – which we are looking at in order to see what work the introduction is doing in each case. They all come from the same book (Ramsden 1988), a collection of essays by different authors on the same theme of improving student learning.

Example 1 begins as follows:

> Computers have been tested for their feasibility as learning aids for approximately two decades now.
>
> (Laurillard 1988: 215)

This introductory sentence is a general statement – presented as fact – about how things are, a situation with which it is assumed the reader will agree. The writer is claiming the right to speak with authority on this matter. This provides a context, or setting, for exploring in detail some particular aspect of that situation in order to pose and answer questions about it. It is as if the chapter will present a close-up view which focuses on a detail in a complete picture. In this case, the discussion will be of how the use of computers as learning aids needs to be rethought in the light of different ways of defining learning and teaching.

Example 2 is the beginning and end of a two-paragraph introduction:

> We stand at an important cross-roads if we wish to take advantage of recent advances to improve learning in secondary schools . . .
> . . . In this chapter I trace the emergence of . . . two [new, important] concepts and their implications for improving learning by reference to a case study . . .
>
> (West 1988: 51)

Again this chapter begins with a general statement – an assertion which the author invites the reader to accept on trust, as the setting for the exploration which is the purpose of the chapter: to 'trace the emergence of two [new] concepts . . .'. Here, then, the introduction tells us both *what* the writer will do in the chapter and *how* (through the case study).

Example 3 is an extract from the first paragraph of another chapter:

> Teaching is a complex phenomenon . . . We would argue that the nature of teaching concerns the relation between the 'teaching situation' and the learning outcome . . .
>
> (Svensson and Hogfors 1988: 162)

The introduction lasts for about one page. It begins with generalizations and explanations about some ideas about teaching and learning that follow from this initial statement, and ends by saying what this chapter will be about: a piece of research that the authors carried out which is based on these ideas.

Finally, here is the first sentence from Example 4:

> A patient is brought to a hospital emergency room suffering from abdominal pain. He looks sick and needs urgent medical attention.
>
> (Welan 1988: 199)

This is a way of interesting the reader with an illustrative example, like a piece of narrative, of the complicated problem of diagnosis which the whole chapter will address. This introduction ends with a statement of what the author intends to do in this chapter and what his argument will be; that is, he announces his central idea, which is what he wants the reader to accept after reading the piece:

> I will argue that by studying how students go about solving diagnostic problems we can learn how to improve our teaching. . . .

You will notice that these four authors are each setting out their own position early on in the chapter. It is as if they are saying: 'this is what we all have to agree before we can go on to talk about our topic'. In particular, they are defining themselves in some way as 'authors' of the piece, in the way we explored in Chapter 9. They all use the first person, 'I' or 'we'.

Writing introductions is not easy. Our examples are written by people who are experienced in the ways of academic writing and whose introductions display both confidence in what they are saying and a sense of self in their work. The reader may never know how unsure the author may be feeling about the work underneath. Example 3, above, is about a project 'that has not been evaluated', but this doesn't prevent the author from writing about it! Nevertheless, this introduction works successfully because the author has decided what the whole piece is about and what she wants to say about it, and that she has a 'right' to say it. Once more it is a matter of making use of your material confidently for your own thought-out purpose. This is another reason for writing the introduction after you have written the whole assignment because by then you have had more of an opportunity to take on the language and thinking of the subject, so that you will be in a better position to write the introduction in a confident way.

These four examples of introductions also illustrate that, even within this one book, in which all the chapters are on the same topic of student learning (which means that the authors all have this interest, although, in fact, they may be from different discipline backgrounds), introductions may work differently to provide the reader with a sense of direction. Remember, however, that we have only given you the flavour of the introduction in these examples, because in fact each lasts for at least one or two paragraphs. There is definitely no rule about how long an introduction should be. It all depends on what work it is doing for the assignment.

In these examples each author has decided on the title, whereas commonly in university assignments you have to 'answer' a question that has been set. In this case, your introduction may refer to the assignment question more directly. You may want to explain at the beginning how you are going to address the assignment and also find a way of establishing your own relationship with both the material and the tutor's response to it that you anticipate. Here are some examples of first sentences from students' approaches to an assignment with the following title: 'Basing your answer on two case studies, discuss how different conceptions of "ill health" affect attitudes to treatment.'

I shall be using two case studies to tackle this question . . .

There are a number of contributory factors to ill health . . .

The term 'ill health' has a wide range of meanings which are culturally determined.

The growing interest in community medicine has had an important impact both on the notion of 'ill health' and on approaches to treatment . . .

In these cases, too, the introduction does a particular job: it sets the scene for the reader and indicates the direction of the rest of the piece.

It is important to bear in mind that you do have a choice about how you introduce your assignment and that there are many different ways of doing it. Some introductions will be much more obvious than others. These will be 'set apart' from the main body of the piece of writing, and will announce the writer's intentions. Other introductions will ignore this, leave out the writer's identity and serve more as a simple beginning or opening, which flows more seamlessly into the rest of the assignment.

In the following activity we ask you to look at a range of examples of introductions in students' assignments on the same topic. The purpose of the task is that you are aware of different ways of introducing an assignment and that you are able to notice how the introduction is working. So do try to work with others on this task so that you can compare one another's work.

Activity Thirty-seven: Comparing introductions to student assignments

Working in pairs or groups compare your introductions to the same assignment. How do they help to provide a 'signpost' to the assignment for the reader? For example, do they refer to the question set and to the rest of the assignment? Do they provide background information?

If you prefer, and if you have some examples of your own different assignments, do the same thing with these introductions.

10.2 Writing the conclusion

The conclusion of a piece of writing is your last opportunity to bring together what you have been saying in a form that will tell your reader, 'This is really where all that I have been saying has been leading; this is what I want you, the reader, to think at the end of my essay'. This final statement must arise out of the piece of writing itself. One piece of advice that writing advisers give is that you don't introduce new information in the conclusion. However, one exception to this is that you might point the way to further work that your piece could lead to.

We have just suggested that you consider writing your introduction last. Now we are also suggesting that it can be useful to draft your conclusion at an early stage in your writing. This can give you a sense of direction, helping you clarify where you are heading and what you have to do in your essay in order to get your reader to your final point. If you can see your destination it can be easier to find a route to get there. Here is the conclusion to Svensson and Hogfors (1988), our third example in the previous section:

> Making the students' conceptions part of the content of teaching would seem to be the most direct way one can achieve an improvement in education.

The whole essay has been devoted to demonstrating this idea, which refers back to the title and which is clearly the chapter's central idea.

How do you make sure that your conclusion doesn't just repeat the introduction? In fact, in a way it might almost seem to do this, except that you will be able to take into account the reader's journey with you through your essay. In many cases it will not. In general terms the work of the conclusion is that it gives a sense of completion to the assignment and points to your central idea. In some cases the conclusion may consist of a summary of the whole piece.

What the conclusion may do

- Summarize the 'answers' to the questions the assignment set out to address, signalled in the introduction.
- Refer back to the question posed in the title and show that it has been answered.
- Give a sense of 'the ending'.
- Point out what the assignment has and has not answered.
- Show that the writer has done what they proposed to do.
- Put forward the writer's point of view in the light of the evidence they have presented.
- Allow the writer to be positive about the ideas in the assignment.
- Point the reader forward to a new related idea.

Activity Thirty-eight: Investigating conclusions

Look for some conclusions in your own work or in any reading you are doing. Check them against the above list. What are these conclusions doing? Do they work well to sum up for the reader the message of the text?

Sometimes conclusions show what the author considers is important, but you need to have read the whole of the essay to understand this. This is why students sometimes think that the conclusion is the place where the writer can express their own opinion. Beware of this idea, however, because the conclusion still has to follow on from the whole piece of writing. You can't spend the whole essay putting two sides of an argument, for example about capital punishment, and then simply say, 'Well, what I think is . . .'. By this stage, you should have built up a case for your point of view, and you will probably have signalled this in the introduction. Then make sure that you follow this through in your conclusion.

Is it necessary to draw a final conclusion? Can't you just stop when you have finished what you want to say? In some subjects it is absolutely expected that the writer makes a definite conclusion. Sometimes, though, especially when you are writing a short piece, it is a good idea to stop when you have said all that you want to say – when you feel you have reached the end of your argument. You may have signposted your way through the piece so that your reader does not need a final 'sum-up' section. Again, remember to fit your work to the task. For the writer who writes according to a 'grand plan' (see Chapter 6), this approach can work. Beware, however – it can mean that you are treating a university assignment more like a journalism article (or a novel) where you can afford to leave things hanging in the air or expect the reader to do more of the work. In university assignments you tend to need to be very explicit and spell things out.

Activity Thirty-nine: Writing your conclusions

Look at two titles of assignments that you might be doing. Note down ideas about what the conclusion could be.

The point of this activity is that you think in a forward kind of way about your ending. When you actually start working on an assignment, try writing out a provisional conclusion at a very early stage. This will be very helpful in clarifying your thinking and in giving you a good sense of achievement and direction.

10.3 Reviewing your work: redrafting and editing

We are linking the terms 'redrafting' and 'editing' in this chapter although, in practice, they are usually thought of as rather different activities. It is usually assumed that redrafting takes place at an earlier stage than editing and that it may involve a more comprehensive rewrite. A first draft could, for example, be a piece of non-stop practice writing in which you quickly write as much as you can of your whole assignment (see Chapter 2). You then rewrite it, and this may involve a lot of change. One way of thinking about the difference between redrafting and editing is that redrafting is usually done by the writer themself when they work towards getting down what they really think they want to say. This may take place throughout the writing process, especially if you are using a computer, which makes it very easy to redraft as you write. Certainly this may be the case if you are the sort of writer who writes in order to find out what you think and where you are with your thinking. Some professional writers say that they redraft many times before they are satisfied. Editing may be seen more as a matter of checking over the organization and style of your work, although you may wish to deal with some content matters at this stage too. It takes place from the perspective of an outsider, even if this outsider is the writer themself. Professional academic writers, offering a paper for an academic journal, have their work read by several 'referees' on behalf of the editor. These readers count as knowledgeable peers and help determine whether or not the article will be published and, if so, what amendments might be useful. In their reading they may well send the writer suggestions as to what does not work or what should be changed.

You will see from this that the kind of individualistic approach that very often applies in student university writing for assessment is not extended to the world of the experienced academic. We believe that it is extremely useful and interesting for students to discuss their work with each other, including their written assignments. You will remember that we introduced this idea in Chapter 5. You learn both from having your piece read and from reading and commenting on others' work. If you think of handing in your work for assessment as similar to submitting it for publication – the point when you make it public – you will see how important the final stage of getting it well presented is, and how getting feedback from others can help to improve it. This feedback should be seen as an essential part of communicating in writing, yet more often than not it is neglected by both students and their tutors. If you think of yourself as a professional – that being a student is your work for the time being – you will want to produce as professional a piece of work as possible. This means that you need to try to read your work before handing it in as if you were an outsider, to see if it is going to be clear, complete and coherent to the reader. At this stage you will be editing your work. We go on to give you some suggestions about ways of checking through your work both on your own and with a 'critical friend' with a view to clarifying it for the reader.

10.4 Editing for the reader

It is important to take account of the reader of your work. The main readers of your assignment will be your tutor and perhaps a 'second marker' and an external examiner. Sometimes students are asked to write 'as if' for a specialist external reader, particularly on professional courses, but even these are usually simulated, rarely 'for real'. This means that writing assignments for university is a strange kind of communication. Although she is your reader, your tutor does not strictly 'need' your work, and usually you can assume that she knows more about the topic than you do. Sometimes the tutor reads your assignment just to give you feedback, but usually assignments are written and read in order to be marked.

This all makes writing for university difficult because it goes against the usual common-sense view of what communication is all about. However, you might find it easier if, as we explored in Chapter 7, you think of your assignment as presenting an argument, which depends not so much on the actual information given in it as the use you make of this information for what you want to say. If you remember that, however much the tutor knows, she does not yet quite know the exact way in which you will argue your case, then it follows that the assignment has to be written so as to be complete – you cannot expect the tutor to fill in the gaps just because you think she 'should know' about what is missing. Students very often find that they have written an assignment which omitted the very thing that was central in their minds, perhaps because they know it so well that they assume that the reader knows it too, or perhaps because they know that they are writing for someone who knows more than they do. However, at the same time, it is also true that you do not need to tell the reader every little detail about what has become public knowledge on the course. As we have stressed before, you should not spend too much space recounting what happened – the point is to make use of this in developing an argument and to avoid the reader reacting along the lines of, 'Yes, true, but so what? Why are you telling me this?'

10.5 Reviewing your work: what are you looking for?

As we have emphasized before, all aspects of writing an assignment can take place at different points. This is equally true of reviewing it. You will certainly need to do this at the end of an assignment, but it is likely that you may well also do it before you reach this final stage. Writing takes place in a spiral mode where you keep going back almost to the same place. So, although we have said that 'reviewing' your work must take place towards the end of the process, in practice you will probably do it at different stages. Beware of spending time on a fine-tune edit before you have at least an overview of the whole piece.

As it is actually very difficult to see your work from the outside, we propose that you try to work with a fellow student at this stage. It will help both of you. Here is a checklist for reviewing your own work. Note that this checklist will be useful for reading someone else's work as well as reading your own as an outsider. Try therefore to work with someone else at this stage, carefully reading each other's work. It does not matter whether or not you have written on the same assignment. The questions below are mainly to find out whether the piece has presented an argument which hangs together around a central idea.

Editing your work as an 'outsider'

- Does the piece of work have a central idea? Is this idea apparent for the reader or do you have to 'search' for it? Is it clear enough for you to restate in a different way?
- Does the piece of work raise any questions that it does not answer?
- Is there a sense of an 'argument' developing?
- Do points – both within and beyond paragraphs – seem to follow logically?
- Does the whole piece hang together?
- Why is a particular bit of information in the piece? What work is it doing for expressing the ideas of the assignment? (For example, is there too much 'chronology writing' at the expense of analysis?)
- Can you understand what is written? If not, can you see why? Does the use of subject terminology seem clear and confident?
- Does the introduction seem helpful as a signpost to the whole piece?
- Is there a sense of a satisfying 'ending'?
- Does the ending in particular, as well as the piece as a whole, answer the question that has been set? How do you know? Has the writer referred to the question clearly and explicitly?

Activity Forty: Checking for 'development of an argument' in an assignment

Choose an assignment. Take each paragraph in turn (if the paragraphs are short it might be best to group two or three together) and write down the main point of each in a list.

The final list should look like an outline for the whole piece of work. If you are doing this for yourself it allows you to check your final piece against your initial plan, to see if you have left anything out or put something in the wrong place. However, please note that it might be the initial plan that was wrong not the final piece.

When you are working with a friend it can also be very helpful both for the one giving and the one receiving feedback to ask for additional comments on what they are concerned about in the particular piece of work. Below are some suggestions for the kinds of question that you might like to ask someone reading your work. Can you add any of your own?

- Does this example work?
- Is this idea clear to you?
- Have I put in too much evidence here?
- Do I seem too personal?
- Is my English 'all right'?

Your constructively critical (but possibly ignorant of the subject) reader could come in with some of their own questions as they read. In Chapter 5 we gave an example of a student's response to another student's work. You may now like to look back at this.

Once you have gone through your assignment in these different ways, you might find that you need to make quite a range of changes which could include: reordering your work; rewriting the introduction or conclusion to include mention of what exactly the assignment is about; cutting out some parts that you have written. Don't necessarily destroy your edited bits because they may come in handy later, perhaps for revision or another piece of work.

10.6 Reorganizing your work: an example

The following short assignment, set in a science foundation course, seemed a fairly simple task: the title, 'The structure of the earth', indicated a description shape for the writing, and the student assumed that his main job was to collect, select and organize the information. He used three encyclopaedias. After he had drafted the piece on a computer, he printed it out and talked it over with a tutor and together they worked out how it could be organized a little differently to make the sequence clearer. The changes he made are indicated by numbers on the text:

The Structure of the Earth

The following essay will give a brief explanation as to the formation of the earth and its position in our solar system. It will also give information on the earth's surface, Crust (outer layer), Mantle (layer below the crust) and Core (the centre), including measurements and sizes.

The earth is the 3rd largest planet from the sun and the fifth largest in our solar system. It was formed approximately five billion years ago. It is believed to have formed from swirling clouds of dust and gases. The inside of the earth is in constant activity, evidence of this is shown on the surface by way of earthquakes, volcanoes, land shifts and subsidence.

The earth is flatter at the poles, north and south, than at the equator. It revolves around the sun at 18.5 million miles per second and takes roughly 365 days to complete a circuit. It also spins on its axis at 1000 miles per hour and takes about 24 hours to complete a rotation.

The earth's surface covers about 197 million sq. Miles. Of this 140 million sq. miles is water and 57 sq miles is land – about 30%. It has an equational circumference of 24, 902 miles , an equatorial radius of 3, 963d miles and a polar radius of 3, 950 miles. It has a mass of 5.976 x 1027 grams and a means density of 5.517 grams per cubic cm. (see chart)

The core consists of an outer and inner part. The outer core starts at about 1800 miles below the crust and is 1400 miles thick. It behaves like a liquid and consists of molten iron. The inner core is 860 miles thick and forms the centre of the earth. Evidence suggests that this inner core consists almost entirely of extremely dense iron and nickel (Collier 1995 p. 478).

The mantle also consists of inner and outer parts. Combined, the mantle extends 1800 miles below the crust and surrounds the core. The upper mantle is 600 miles thick and the lower mantle 1200 miles thick. The mantle is composed of dense magnesium iron silicates. This in turn forms rocks such as peridotite, dunite, and eclogite. During natural mountain forming, pieces of crust are pushed down through to the upper mantle. Due to the heat, this is melted and eventually sent back to the crust surface via volcanic eruptions, the lava sometimes contains rock material from the mantle produced by the iron silicates.

The crust is basically the skin of the earth. It only accounts for 5 percent of the earth's thickness. It comes in two forms continental and oceanic. The continental crust is rich in silica and alumina minerals. The oceanic crust is of a silica magnesia composition. Due to the processes of nature some of the continental crust is becoming oceanic and vice versa. The crust's thinnest points can be found under the oceans, between three and five miles thick. The oceans form

Handwritten annotations in margins:
1. cut
This essay, 2.
will...
3. Background
cut 4
'surface' 5
'core'
8
Move around 7 'mantle'
'crust'
6 Move
PTO

roughly two thirds of the earth's surface, of which there are three main sections:
the pacific, the atlantic and the indian. The continents form the other third of
the earth's surface and are divided into seven parts. Most of these continents are
found in the northern hemisphere.

  In fact there is still a great deal to learn about the earth's formation
and its compositions. Technology has not yet been developed to explore the earth's
core. At present we have only been able to examine the outer part of the mantle.
Also, because we know very little about the earth's beginning, we cannot get any
pointers as to the exact materials that made the planet what it is today. This is
in total contrast to what we know about the earth surface. This is obviously
because we are in contact with the earth's surface daily.

He decided to omit the first sentence because it suggested that the essay was about the formation and position of the earth (1). This was background but not central information. The central point of the essay was the earth's structure. However, he kept the following paragraph (3) as background and context. He turned the second sentence into an introductory sentence and added mention of the surface (2). He decided to omit the third paragraph as irrelevant for his topic (4). Then he rearranged the rest of his information about each part of the earth that he was discussing, to put it in the same order as in his introduction: the earth's crust (6) comes after the surface (5), then the earth's mantle (7) and finally the core (8). This is a logical progression from the earth's surface inwards.

As a result of his reorganization the student can now finish his assignment with a conclusion to sum up what is still unknown, and here he makes a general contrast between knowledge about the earth's surface and the rest of its structure, really bringing together the different parts of his piece to make his general point about why this is so: 'We are in contact with the earth's surface daily'.

Although the above example is obviously a very simple and short piece of written work – in fact, it was an introductory course assignment – it should help you to see how you can move things about to change the emphasis of ideas in your writing. We hope that overall this chapter has made you think about both the different ways in which you can approach editing and redrafting your work and the flexibility available to you as a writer when using introductions and conclusions.

Notes

- Notice if you are repeating yourself, but bear in mind that repetition is sometimes necessary in order to remind the reader of something you have said before.

- Consider writing the introduction after you have completed the rest of the essay.
- Don't be afraid to cut when you are reviewing your work. You can keep these cuts to use later.
- Think carefully about the particular work your introduction and conclusion are doing.
- Ask someone else to read your work at the editing stage.
- Try to leave at least 24 hours between completing and reviewing your assignment.

11

Completing the assignment and preparing for next time

Grammar and punctuation • Techniques for working on your writing •
Handing in your assignment • Learning from feedback: grades and
tutors' comments

The feedback on my essay says that I have problems with my grammar and
punctuation. What does that mean?

Your writing is incoherent. I cannot follow your argument.

There seems to be no linkage between your ideas.

11.1 Grammar and punctuation

Until now we have not made a specific point of talking about grammar and
punctuation in your written work. In our experience academic staff sometimes focus too much on these particular concepts when they are talking about
problems with writing, and students themselves often panic about their own

feelings of insecurity in this area and lack confidence writing in formal written English styles. Consequently, we have waited until later in the book to start talking about checking your work for grammatical difficulties and misleading punctuation. We hope that, if you have worked through the book, by this stage you will feel more confident about yourself as a university writer and are less likely to see that the problems you have with writing are primarily concerned with grammar and punctuation.

You may remember that in Chapter 1 we asked you to think about your own linguistic history and the dialects and languages that you had been more used to using before embarking upon university studies. This implicit knowledge about language is what you draw on when you are deciding how to write. Although you may think that you do not know about the rules of grammar, everybody who speaks or writes a language intuitively knows the rules of grammar of that language. You may, in fact, speak a number of different languages or dialects in addition to the formal English styles that you are most likely to use for your writing for university. In this case, you will be a competent user of a number of different grammars. What you may not know is how to describe the rules of these grammars explicitly, using the specific words that linguists and others use to describe the constituent parts of a sentence. What we hope to do in this section is to draw on your intuitive grammatical knowledge to help you to check your own work.

11.2 Techniques for working on your writing

We are going to concentrate on examining four key concepts from language studies to help you work on your own writing: cohesion; punctuation; reference; and coherence. Note that 'reference' in this context is not the same as 'referencing sources'.

Cohesion

Cohesion is concerned with the way in which parts of written texts fit together to make a whole rather than a series of disconnected bits. This is particularly important when you are writing an assignment, and you need to pay attention to the connecting devices that you use. These devices connect the ideas in one sentence to the previous sentence and to the following sentence. They also connect the smaller parts of the sentence together, the phrases and clauses. In the same way, they connect paragraphs to each other. The connecting devices help to carry your argument along and lend structure to your writing, so that the reader finds it easier to understand. Connecting devices link all the different parts of your writing together so that it makes sense, not just to you but to anybody who is going to read your assignment. When you use connecting devices you will be relying on your intuitive knowledge of grammar in knowing which words fit together and in what kind of order, so that everything makes sense. Reading aloud gives you a sense of how well the connections are working.

You can think about cohesion in your writing at different levels, in terms of connections between topics; themes; words and phrases, as in the examples below:

Connecting topics

I give presentations from mind maps and sometimes hand them out. They're more visually exciting than linear notes.
(The writer connects mind maps + linear notes)

There are examples of societies whose violence is based on social ties and others where violent warfare is seen as a stabilizing force on the community. Even apparently peaceful groups such as the Buid or Inuit Eskimos experience some levels of violence in their close communities.
(The writer connects violence in society + peaceful groups)

Connecting themes

In the extract from the student essay in Chapter 5, notice the three themes of the paragraphs:

- theories of child language acquisition;
- areas of evidence;
- theoretical perspectives.

Connecting words and phrases

Then	Firstly, secondly
However	In contrast
Despite	In addition
Consequently	An example of
Nevertheless	Similarly
Therefore	Clearly
Yet	But
Although	And
Because	As a result
Since	

Activity Forty-one: Checking for cohesion

Take a piece of your own written work. Read the text aloud. Pause at the end of each sentence. Ask yourself the following questions:

- Does the sentence make complete sense?
- Does it relate to the sentence which went before? How?
- Does it relate to the sentence which follows? How?
- Are too many ideas embedded in one sentence?
- How are the paragraphs related to each other?
- Does each paragraph introduce a new theme?
- How are new ideas introduced?
- Do they relate to other parts of the text?
- Look out for the connecting devices listed above.

Punctuation

When we speak we can help the listener to understand through the use of gestures, facial expressions and body language. We can also use pauses, hesitations and repetitions to add to the force of what we are saying and to make sure that the listener has understood what we are trying to communicate. When we are writing we have to use different mechanisms to do the same work. This is where punctuation comes in. It allows us to divide up our ideas into manageable chunks so that the reader understands what we are trying to say. There are many different rules and conventions regarding punctuation but even following these norms you still have flexibility in the use of a variety of punctuation marks. Many students feel anxious about the use of punctuation in their writing. If you feel this way, it may help to consider punctuation as an aid to enable you, as the writer, to make your writing as clear as possible.

It may seem strange to think about punctuation as a cohesive device when, on the surface, it looks as if punctuation breaks your writing up. By breaking up the writing into chunks and creating different weighting of importance for the parts of your writing, punctuation actually makes connections so that the writing begins to take on an overall structure. Punctuation relies on certain conventions, but it is often very difficult to describe the rules that are used. What we attempt to do here is to talk about the most common forms of punctuation that students have difficulties with and the ones that will be most beneficial to practise using in your assignment writing. It is important to remember that effective use of different forms of punctuation is an asset. It should be a help rather than a hindrance with your writing. The most useful starting point is to pay attention to the ways in which the authors that you read use punctuation in their writing.

The most commonly used punctuation marks which students have difficulties with are full stops, commas, colons, semicolons and apostrophes. We
suggest that you read through the examples below to see if you know how to
incorporate these into your own work. Then you can complete Activity Forty-
two at the end of this section, which is designed to help you identify the
different uses of these punctuation marks.

Full stops

Full stops signal the end of a sentence. They indicate that the writer has completed one complete thought or idea. A full stop can come at the end of a
simple or a complex sentence:

> Emily finished her book.

> She did not want to begin the piece of work until she had finished reading
> her book.

> Normally, Emily liked to begin writing before she had actually finished
> her research but on this occasion she wanted to be sure that first she
> completely understood what she had been reading.

Although these example sentences differ in their complexity, they all contain
a complete thought on the part of the writer. The best way that you can make
sure that you are writing in complete sentences and using full stops correctly is
to read your work aloud. This will help you to decide if it makes sense.

Commas

Using commas effectively can be quite difficult. Students often feel confused
about where to put commas in their writing. One of the reasons for this is
that conventions for their use vary depending on the writer and the context. If
you are beginning to write for a new subject you may find it easier if you use
shorter sentences to begin with. This can make it easier to order your ideas and
therefore to use commas more effectively. The following sentences give some
examples of the situations in which you will find yourself needing to use
commas:

> The strange, disturbing, eerie silence was interrupted by a ghostly scream.

> The author, who writes about the changing perceptions of childhood in
> the early twentieth century, gives numerous examples to illustrate her
> theoretical position.

> However, in practice many students do find writing assignments a difficult
> and daunting process but gradually they begin to develop their own
> identity as writers and this gives them an increasing sense of satisfaction.

In the first example, the commas are used to separate similar words (adjectives) which are used to describe another word (a noun). When we write a list of adjectives in front of a noun we use commas to separate the adjectives. It is not usual to put a comma between the final adjective and the word that it is describing.

In the second example, the words between the commas add meaning to the rest of the sentence. Using commas in this way enables the writer to use additional material in the same sentence and to elaborate on her original thought.

In the third example, the first word is followed by a comma because it stands alone as a form of introduction to the new sentence. In fact, in a grammatical sense it is making a connection to the sentence which went before and creating cohesion in the text. It is common to put a comma after words used in this way.

If you read a piece of writing aloud you will begin to hear that certain words are connected to one another. These linkages enable us to make sense of what we hear and what we read. As with all punctuation, the purpose of commas is to help the reader separate the text into readable chunks, and if you insert punctuation marks in inappropriate places then this makes it more difficult for the reader to make sense of what you are writing. You may inadvertently separate words which need to be connected to make sense of the text. This is why the process of reading your own work aloud is so valuable.

Semicolons

Semicolons have two common uses. First, they are used to separate items in a list after a colon (see the section below on the colon). Second, they can indicate a particular kind of relationship and connection between two parts of a sentence. They are useful to use when the second part of the sentence is still integrally related to the first; in such a case, the use of a full stop would appear too final. At the same time, if you use a semicolon you are indicating a more important break within a sentence than you would if you just used a comma. A semicolon can also be used instead of 'and' when you are connecting two parts of a sentence:

> It was snowing rather heavily; the girl pulled her coat tightly around her to keep out the cold.

Long sentences tend to cause the most problems with punctuation, as in the following:

> In long sentences a number of different aspects of one idea can be expressed, and these can give the writer the opportunity to elaborate upon what it is that she wants to say; if the writer begins to lose the thread that

she started out with at the beginning of the sentence, then punctuation can help to create a kind of order.

The sentence above is 62 words long and the writer has just about got away with keeping the sense of what she is trying to say. In this case, the use of the comma and semicolon are useful aids to helping the reader along. Alternatively, the writer could have chosen to express her ideas in two shorter sentences. One problem with consistently using shorter sentences is that you may find this a limitation if you are trying to express more complex ideas.

Colons

Traditionally, the colon is used within a sentence when the second part of the sentence expands upon the first:

In practice, the use of colons is less common than it used to be: in many instances the semicolon or the full stop are used where in the past writers would have been more likely to use a colon.

Another use of the colon is to introduce a list and the items in the list are then separated by semicolons:

Emily liked to get everything that she needed together before she started reading and taking notes: paper; a pencil; different coloured pens; highlighters; sticky notes.

Colons are also used to introduce a separate part of a text such as a short quote. You will find examples of this usage throughout this book.

Apostrophes

Many students feel confused about the use of apostrophes and play safe in their writing by leaving them out. Although the meaning is unlikely to be lost if you do not know how to use apostrophes, as with other forms of punctuation they do have a purpose and do help the reader to make sense of your writing. Consequently, it is worth spending a few minutes making sure that you know how to use apostrophes in your own writing. Again, look out for how they are used in the books and articles that you read.

One of the most common confusions that students experience with apostrophes is the distinction between *its* and *it's*. This causes a lot of difficulties for students because the two forms look so similar but actually have completely different meanings.

It's is a contraction (a shortened version) of 'it is'. Instead of writing 'it is' in full the 'i' of 'is' is omitted and an apostrophe used in its place. Contractions are common in English and replace parts of the verbs 'to be' and 'to have' which have been omitted:

- *there's* (there is, there has)
- *they're* (they are)
- *we're* (we are)
- *they've* (they have)

In contrast, *its* (without an apostrophe) denotes ownership or possession.

> The bird went into its nest.
>
> Everything has its rightful place.

What can seem confusing is the fact that with other words ending in 's' we often use an apostrophe to indicate possession (bird's nest). The apostrophe in this case is being used instead of saying 'the nest of the bird'; it is a kind of shorthand. The apostrophe placed before the final 's' is the singular possessive form (bird's nest) and the apostrophe placed after the 's' is the plural possessive form (birds' nests).

As you write your assignments you will probably find that the same words occur repeatedly which you find confusing with regard to the use of the apostrophe. Look out for words that you frequently find yourself having difficulties with, such as these:

- child's
- children's
- women's
- men's
- proper names (Elizabeth's)
- theirs

Also remember to look out for the situations when you do not use an apostrophe, when nouns are being used in their plural form:

> Nowadays *girls* seem to be more successful than *boys* at every level of the education system. There is also some evidence that male *students* are falling behind their female counterparts in higher education and more women than men are now becoming *doctors* and *lawyers*. In many different situations men seem to be experiencing a change in their traditional *roles*.

Activity Forty-two: Looking at punctuation

Take a page of a book or article that you are reading for your studies at the moment. Identify the punctuation marks listed above.

- Why do you think the author used this form of punctuation?
- How would the text have read if some of the punctuation marks were changed or left out altogether?
- Now look at a page of your own writing. How have you used punctuation marks? Have you used similar conventions?

Reference

Reference is concerned with the ways in which different parts of the text refer to one another. When we are writing we often substitute different words and phrases when we talk about the same subject or topic again. This is how we create a sense of reference in the text. One of the more common ways of doing this is to substitute pronouns such as, 'she', 'he', 'it' for the person or thing previously mentioned by name. A simple example would be 'Pat is coming but she will be late'. The concept of reference is, in a sense, what makes written texts more interesting. Instead of saying the same thing again and adding to it, we use many different forms of reference to talk about and extend topics that have already been mentioned. The idea of reference also depends upon an implicit understanding of the writer that the reader has some knowledge of what the writer is saying. Writers rely upon all sorts of assumptions concerning the reader's knowledge about their writing. This enables writers to avoid repetition and leave out what may seem like irrelevant information. When you are checking your work you need to pay attention to the words which carry this sense of reference and hold the different parts of your writing together. You will need to think about the words that refer backwards and forwards within the text. Look out for words used as substitutes for other words. Do they make sense and actually refer to the person or thing that you the writer intend? It is very easy to end up writing so that words such as these can have an ambiguous meaning. When reference words are used to substitute for words or phrases that you have already used in the text, you need to check that they do in fact refer in the way that you, the writer, intended. The following list indicates words that are commonly used to make reference to other parts of the text:

its
his
her
he

she
they
their
this
that
those
these
it

Activity Forty-three: Checking connections and reference

Look at the extract from the student essay below. Can you pick out any connecting devices, words, topics and themes? Can you pick out any referring words? Do the same exercise on a piece of your own work.

Many arguments have been put forward suggesting that violence is an innate quality in human beings: a state of nature which cannot be avoided. Sahlins argued that violence occurs in an absence of the state to which the tribe was seen as a forerunner (Harrison 1989). In contrast, he made parallels between a state of nature and war which depended on a lack of social ties and others where violent warfare is seen as a stabilizing force on the community. However, there is evidence to suggest that this hypothesis is inaccurate. There are examples of societies whose violence is based on social ties and others where violent warfare is seen as a stabilizing force on the community. Even apparently peaceful groups such as the Buid or Inuit Eskimos experience some levels of violence in their close communities. Before any discussion of the topic it is important to realize that violence and aggression are Western concepts and in other cultures things that we may perceive as violent can be justified as acceptable, necessary or the work of spiritual powers. In contrast, other societies may see unacceptable levels of violence and aggression in activities that we see as part of everyday life.

Coherence

Coherence is really concerned with the overall sense of your written text. Having read aloud and checked the sense of individual words and sentences as you go, you need to find out if the whole assignment is coherent and has a clear structure which your reader will be able to recognize as they read through your work. Probably if you are not sure what to put in and what to leave out it is best to err on the safe side and put in the information that *you* feel is necessary to make the text coherent. Cohesion and reference are both elements of creating a coherent text. When you write you will unconsciously take account of all the different concepts that we have tried to unpack in this chapter so far. Your own intuitive knowledge of grammar and the way in which sentences work and are structured will help you to realize when things are not making sense. You may need to rewrite some parts of your assignment to make sure that it is more coherent. You may move parts around or change the organization of the paragraphs. The way in which your final piece of work is divided into paragraphs will depend upon the subject matter which you are dealing with in your assignment. In general, as you move on to a completely new topic or new theme of a topic you will start a new paragraph. Paragraphs which are very short can be rather disjointed to read. Those which are very long can lose the reader in a sea of different ideas. Paragraphs are there to break up the text into manageable chunks for both reader and writer. You may find that headings help as signposts for both you and the reader and can help to make the text coherent. You can check with your tutor if she or he likes the use of headings in written assignments. Again, our advice is to pay attention to the things that you are reading as their use varies from subject to subject.

Activity Forty-four: Working on your finished assignment

Take your own finished assignment. Read it through aloud, paying attention to the issues that we have covered in this section: cohesion; reference; coherence.

- Does the finished piece of writing make sense?
- Are there any parts that you feel unsure about?
- Do you need to do any rewriting or final editing before handing in the finished piece?

11.3 Handing in your assignment

We have now come to the end of the process of writing your assignment. This will be the point when you will present your assignment to your tutor – and when it is no longer yours. You hand it over and are ready to get on with the next piece of work. At this point you have to accept that you have done the best you can in the time and with the resources available to you. You might bear in mind a piece of advice an artist once gave his pupil: 'Remember that the worst paintings of all are the ones you never paint.' It is not, in fact, quite the end of the matter – you will get some kind of feedback, and in the final part of this chapter we will be making suggestions about how to use that feedback. In some cases, depending on the practices in your university, you may not get your original piece of work back. For this reason and also because it has been known for students' work to get lost in the system, do keep a spare copy. You will need it for your own records, and you may also want to use your assignment for revising for exams later on. If you have put a lot of work into an assignment, finally handing it in can be rather a strange feeling. You may feel that you could have done better, or that you can't tell how it will be judged by your tutor. The fact that you are doing an assignment which will be graded affects your feelings about your work considerably. You may realize at this stage that what your tutor will say about the work will only partly depend on how much work you have put into the piece. Students vary enormously in the amount of time and effort they put into a piece of work and you may find that some assignments are done relatively quickly, while others take an unexpectedly long time to complete. We hope that this book helps you to make the best use of the time you spend in preparing an assignment by thinking about different parts of the process and by helping you to understand what is involved for you in writing. However, in the end how much time you spend on it will depend on many different factors, which you will need to work out for yourself as you gain experience of writing assignments.

11.4 Learning from feedback: grades and tutors' comments

You will get some kind of feedback on your work from your tutor, although how much and in what form will vary enormously. In some cases, you will just get a grade or a percentage mark. This is most likely to be the case when your writing has been done at the end of a course or a unit. The grade may feel like the most important kind of feedback you could get: it gives you a point of comparison with other students and it tells you if you have passed this stage. It validates you as a student. It can also cause you disappointment if you thought you deserved better, especially if you have put a lot of work into the assignment.

What do grades mean? First, it is important to know that there is no complete agreement in grading written assignments. It is not just a matter of counting points. Different tutors can mark differently and the same tutor may mark differently at different times. Having a second marker helps to ensure some consistency, but tutors will give their own emphasis to the different elements of a written assignment. Second, grading is about some external university standard and unfortunately does not usually take your own progress into account. Therefore, try not to get too caught up in your grades if you are in your first year, as these are most unlikely to count towards your final results. You may need to pass to ensure that you can proceed to the next stage of the course, but this is all for now. If you are not too concerned you will be more likely to feel free to experiment with new ways of working, develop your own style and methods, and tackle more demanding assignments. Although you may be disappointed to receive a lower grade than you hoped for a piece of work, in the long run a low grade may be more beneficial to you. It may make you stop and think and read the feedback to see what your tutor has to say about what went wrong. It may also mean that you take the time to go and see your tutor and ask their advice on what to do next time. With a high grade you may be tempted to forget to look at the feedback altogether, but it is important that you pay attention to the feedback even if you have done really well. Your tutor's feedback should still be able to help you next time.

There may be a statement on your course about what the different grades mean, although it is not always easy to apply such information. Almost always you will find that the higher grades are given for analysis, relevance to the question and the ability to think critically, whereas low pass grades are given for being descriptive, and for just giving information without selection, organization or argument.

Using written feedback

If your assignment is returned to you, it is a very good idea to review your work at that point. You may not feel like doing this because it now feels as if it is all in the past, but it is a good way to develop and build on what you have done. If you have not managed to talk with a fellow student before, try to do so now. Read each other's assignments and compare and discuss any comments you have received. This is also useful because it is not always easy to know what a tutor means. In order to understand written comments you often already have to have a feel for the conventions of the subject or of academic writing more generally. So, talking this over with other students will help. It can also be difficult to know what to do with the comments you receive. Some tutors can find it difficult to understand the problems that students have with writing, so that their advice is sometimes well intentioned but difficult to put into practice. Again, discuss this with another student or with your tutor.

Talking with a tutor

On some courses tutors offer tutorials to discuss students' assignments. It is up to you to make good use of these – for instance, by rereading your assignment before you see the tutor and by identifying any feedback or issue that you would like to have your tutor's opinion on. Tutors conduct these tutorials in their own way, but they too will find it easier if you are prepared and know what you want from them. Some tutors offer sessions, either individually or in groups, on assignment drafts and outlines, which are more obviously developmental for your writing. It is really important to make good use of talking with your tutor even though you may now have moved on to other work. Tutors are your best source of expertise on writing in their subject area.

Understanding tutors' written comments

The written feedback on your assignment should help you to understand why you got a particular grade and also help you to do better next time. Tutors vary enormously in how much feedback they give students, and written feedback can be quite individual. Increasingly courses use 'feedback sheets', pro formas with headings, to break down how you have done into different categories. If your course does not use one of these, then you need to attend carefully to the comments in the margin and at the end of the piece of work.

The following are examples of tutors' comments:

- You need to develop an argument.
- This essay lacks structure.
- I need a clear introduction telling me where you are going.
- I cannot see your reading.
- Could you clarify this point?
- More analysis of this point is necessary.

Comments like these will probably seem familiar to you, but the question is how you actually make sense of them and use them in your next piece of written work. As we have said, it is important to pay attention to the feedback and not just to the grade that you have got for your assignment. The feedback should help to point you in the direction of what went wrong (and, of course, right) in this assignment and how you can build on what you have learnt for next time. The way in which you can use feedback depends a little on how your course is structured. If you are following a modular course in which all your writing is assessed, then you may find that you do not get back your written work, and hence your feedback, until you have finished the module. In this case, it can be more difficult for you to put your feedback to good use for the next piece of writing. In general, assignments should be returned during the duration of a particular course, so that you are in a position to draw on feedback for next time.

The feedback that you get is likely to deal with both the content of the assignment and the way in which you have written this content: broadly speaking, comments referring to 'argument', 'structure', 'clarity', 'analysis' and 'meaning' would be part of the latter. The content comments will tend to be more specific to the piece of writing and less generalizable to other pieces of written work. If you are interested in learning for next time, then you need to concentrate on those comments which deal with the ways in which you have written your central idea and argument and put your themes together. These comments should give you some clues to writing further assignments. If you do not understand the feedback comments, then you should make every effort to follow this up and ask the tutor concerned. Tutors tend to use their own shorthand and have their own personal preferences for how you should be writing. Comments such as those below may be well meaning but are very difficult to unpack if you want to make use of them:

- Meaning?
- Replace this.
- Clarify this point.
- Evaluate.
- Can you say more?

We cannot really stress enough how essential it is that you ask if you don't understand. Another useful strategy, as we have already suggested, is to compare your feedback with that of other students. This can be a helpful way of understanding how the tutor wanted the question to be answered.

Activity Forty-five: Learning from feedback

Look at the feedback that you have received on one of your assignments. Try to identify the comments that deal with this particular assignment and those that are more generalizable to future assignments. Which comments would help you for next time?

You will remember that in Chapter 3 we talked about writing for different disciplines; you will probably find that the kinds of feedback and the emphasis given to particular areas vary between your courses. Feedback from one course may not help you if your next piece of writing is in a different subject area. If possible, discuss this with the tutor or lecturer teaching your new course before you begin your written work. You need to establish if there are any criteria for writing which are specific to the new course and which you may not have come across before in your previous studies. Increasingly, students are given guidelines for writing assignments and 'criteria' statements as to what would make the assignment effective. Again, if you are able to follow these it should help you to get a good mark. However, this is not always as easy as it might seem, because such 'advice' can seem too prescriptive and not sufficiently in line with what you are trying to do to be useful. All the same, take good note of such guidance and use it as you can. If there are no such guidelines and you are embarking on a new course in an unfamiliar subject area, then, as we have said, it is probably worth asking your tutor what they will be looking for in your written work, so that you have some idea of what to attend to when you are writing.

Notes

- Pay attention to the ways in which the authors that you read use punctuation in their writing.

- Ask a friend to read your work and check that it all makes sense.
- Read aloud in order to check your grammar and punctuation for the ways in which they affect the meaning.
- Make every effort to ask your tutor if you don't understand their feedback.
- Try to use something from your feedback to help you improve your next piece of writing.

12

Exploring different kinds of writing

Case study: one student's experience • Report writing • Dissertations and projects • Electronic writing • Using the Internet as a resource for writing • Evaluating web resources • Visual and written texts

I have never written a report before.

I never really know who I am writing for.

I never know how to use something I've got from the Internet.

Up to this point we have been talking mostly about essay writing. This is because essays still tend to be the most common kind of assignments that students are set in higher education. It is also the type of writing that students seem to find particularly difficult and ask the most questions about. However, as we have said already, essays are not the only kind of writing that you will come across during your studies. In this chapter we will try to help you to recognize and address the different kinds of writing that you will be doing, including writing online.

The variety of writing that you will do at university depends very much on your course of study. In the past, when students undertook 'traditional' degrees, they often followed a single subject of study – for example, psychology. This meant that they were able to build upon the writing they did in their first year and perfect this during their second and third years as an undergraduate. It was also the case that many students, particularly in the social sciences and humanities, only *ever* wrote essays. They never had to do any other types of writing, such as report writing. However, today's students often take inter-disciplinary modules which draw on a range of disciplinary perspectives. In these circumstances it is much more difficult to work out what is required for your written work. Additionally, increasing numbers of students now follow vocational and professional courses – for example, nursing, business studies, tourism and leisure.

So, to summarize, there are a number of reasons why you might find yourself being asked to do different types of writing:

• Modular degree structures involving courses not necessarily building one upon the other.
• Interdisciplinary modules (e.g. childhood studies, sports sciences).
• Increasing opportunities for professional and vocational courses.
• The use of different kinds of assessment from the traditional essay (e.g. report writing, summaries, project reports).

Activity Forty-six: Different subjects and different writing

Think about the kind of degree you are taking:

• Is it a single-subject degree?
• Do you study modules in more than one subject?
• Is it an interdisciplinary degree in which the things you study come from a number of different disciplines?
• Is it primarily a vocational degree which prepares you for a particular career?
• Do you have to do different kinds of writing in the courses that make up your degree?
• Make a list of the kinds of writing you have to do for your studies.

You will remember that right at the beginning of this book we said that writing and learning are inseparable. This is why we are asking you to think about the kind of subjects and courses you are studying, and which disciplines or professions are most influential within them. You might also remember us saying that different disciplines can be seen as different ways of viewing the world. Sometimes we talk about a 'disciplinary lens', meaning that a discipline looks at the world in particular ways. The same can be said for professions; both disciplines and professions have their own ways of talking about and understanding the world. Part of the way in which academics and profes-sionals view the world is represented by the way in which they write. As a student, nobody will be expecting you to write like an experienced academic or a well-qualified professional, but they *will* be expecting you to take some account of what particular types of writing in that discipline or profession look like. This is why you are likely to find yourself being asked to do different types of writing as you move between and across courses and disciplines. Becoming familiar with a new subject area means getting to grips with the ways in which people write in that area, and in a small way this is what you are being asked to do as a student.

In order to help you think about the writing you will have to do, we concentrate in this chapter on different types of writing. We begin with a case study of one undergraduate student and look at some of the different kinds of writing that she found herself having to do for assessment. This is a very specific example of one student who was studying for a degree in anthropology and archaeology, but it has relevance for other courses which expect a variety of writing. Although on the face of it this student was only studying two courses, you will see that the kinds of writing that she was doing were in fact very different from each other. We illustrate this with some extracts from her coursework. We suggest that you read through the examples and use these as a basis for thinking about the writing you have to do for your courses.

12.1 Case study: one student's experience

Example 1: A practical report

Archaeology of early societies: a practical report
  What the student said about this:

> I'd never written anything like this archaeological report before I came to university, so I just had to try and make some sort of judgement about what was needed and follow that track. My tutor had some examples of past reports he showed us, and also we all discussed it together on our course. With this kind of report they always ask us to answer particular questions, and so I sort of got a feel for what they were wanting by looking at the kinds of questions that were being asked. We also did some preparation in class first, and the ways that people were talking gave me some ideas about how to write it out. These reports always ask questions and want direct, short answers. I found that difficult to do. It was also the first time I had had to put in diagrams and tables.

Extract from 'Archaeology of early societies: a practical report':

Stratigraphic and sedimentological reinterpretation of Buckfastleigh Cave, South Devon.

Q1. What is the true stratigraphic sequence? i.e. Which is the oldest deposit, which the youngest and in what order did the deposits in

between accumulate? Furthermore, was the deposition of sediment continuous or can major breaks (unconformities) in deposition be observed?

In order to understand the stratigraphic sequence we need to understand the law of superimposition which basically maintains that, in stratigraphy, the deposit lying on top will be younger than the one underneath, as deposits are laid down over time, one on top of the other. Although there are circumstances where this is not the case, the vast majority of the time this law does apply.

In order to record the stratigraphic information in a coherent manner we use a Harris matrix which shows the relationship between each layer. Here is the Harris matrix for Buckfastleigh Cave:

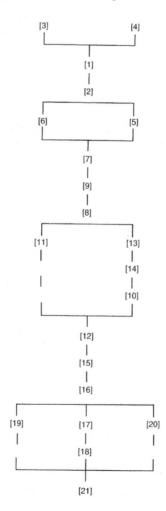

So we can see that the most recent unit was either unit 3 or unit 4 but as they are not directly related to each other we put them on the same level. Unit 1 is the next most recent unit so it comes beneath units 3 and 4. The matrix continues according to these rules.

The deposition of the different layers would not have been continuous. Different layers were laid down in different ways, some over a long period of time and others much more quickly. The sharp breaks between the different strata suggest a sharp change rather than a continuous deposition.

Comment

This is a very particular kind of report which seems to be specifically designed for assessment, with its question and answer format. Later in this chapter we will be looking at other kinds of report writing, which are more similar to professional reports. Notice the way in which this student has to make use of both writing and a diagram (the Harris matrix) together. The written and visual parts of the text are both important in this report format.

Example 2: A collaborative writing project

Boards of resistance: skater-space and the spectacle of a subculture in Bristo Square
    What the student said about this:

> *Three of us did this project together. We took lots of photos because this helped us to visualize the space that we were writing about. We all found the collaborative writing difficult because we really wanted it to have one voice. Because there were three of us writing this we found it difficult to make it coherent. When you are writing on your own it's much easier to have a direct angle on something than when you are writing together. On the other hand, although it is difficult writing with lots of people it does help you think about things in other ways because everyone approaches things differently.*

Extract from 'Boards of resistance: skater-space and the spectacle of a subculture in Bristo Square':

The space
We chose to study Bristo Square because of the large numbers of skateboarders that practise there. Bristo Square is the only place where skaters (and likewise rollerbladers and bikers) can practise freely in central Edinburgh. The nearest skatepark is in Livingston, but in the past 20 years Bristo Square has become the focus of skateboarding activity and social interaction in the city.

The square is located in the centre of Edinburgh within the university complex. It comprises of a slightly sloping paved area of approximately 20 metres square surrounded by wide ascending steps creating an arena effect. There are five entrances to the square, but apart from this it is a relatively enclosed space. In the south-west corner of the square stands a monument (see Fig. 1).

Figure 1 An aerial view of Bristo Square taken from the north-east

The square is primarily used by young males, whose ages range from 8 to 25 years (although the majority fall into the 13–18 age range). These boys use the square for the recreational activities of skateboarding, biking (on BMX bikes) and rollerblading. The skateboarders are by far the largest group using the square and as such they dominate the space. The square is also used by the wider public, in particular students, who sit on the steps at the sides, often whilst eating lunch. Pedestrians regularly cross through the square. A number of teenage girls also frequent the square, often to watch the boys, although a small number do participate in the activities of skateboarding and rollerblading.

Comment

Although the students wrote this project together one cannot detect their different voices. One interesting thing is the way in which they have used a photograph to do some of the work that a written text normally does. This is something that we are unlikely to find in a traditional essay. Although there is some description of the square and its occupants in the text, the picture does a lot of the work for the reader, so that the students do not have to rely solely on their descriptive powers.

Example 3: A review of an article

The transition between hunting and gathering and the specialized husbandry of resources: a socio-ecological approach (Layton et al. 1991).
   What the student said about this:

> When I did this review of an article I found that I partly summarized it and partly analysed it. I tried to put in what I thought were the important things that the authors were saying. It felt different from an essay because I didn't feel that I was trying to develop an argument.

Extract from 'The transition between hunting and gathering and the specialised husbandry of resources: a socio-ecological approach' – Robert Layton, Robert Foley and Elizabeth Williams:

> In this article evidence is put forward to show that there is not a unilinear evolutionary transition from hunting and gathering to intensive husbandry, but that these are simply examples of different subsistence strategies chosen by people to offer them the most productive way of life. The authors emphasize the point that population growth is not a cause of intensive husbandry, but a consequence. These main ideas are illustrated through looking at a variety of alternative subsistence strategies which can be found in the present ethnographic record. They examine not only the 'classic' hunter-gatherer society, but also the 'grey areas' of subsistence strategies, more specifically cases of symbiosis, mixed economies and reversion. The cases of reversion in particular are intended to challenge evolutionary preconceptions. Layton et al. also want to provide alternatives to the traditional reasons for transitions to agriculture (particularly in the Near East). They suggest that technology, climate, natural genetic changes in plants and animals and socio-economic change are important factors, unlike population pressure which they criticize as a model. However, there are certain problems with their arguments. The case made for technology is the weakest as the ethnographic examples cited are examples of introduction rather than innovation and so have limited relevance to transition to intensive husbandry in the Middle East. They argue that the key issue is socio-economic; if a society is not in the right frame of mind, agriculture will not occur despite all other factors.

Comment

The student starts off by summarizing the main arguments put forward by the authors. She then goes on to challenge some of these ideas. In her interview about this piece of work she described it as analysis rather than the development of her own argument, as she would be doing in an essay.

Example 4: A tutorial presentation

What the student said about this:

> When I have to give a tutorial presentation I always write it up beforehand. I wrote this in a very different way from other things I have to write. I tried to write it as if I was explaining something to people who knew nothing. With an essay I might say something in one or two sentences. But with a tutorial presentation you have to explain things a lot more and the same thing applies when you write it up so that you can hand it in. I tend to use the same explanation in the writing up as I do when I give the presentation. When writing an essay you assume a certain amount of knowledge from the person reading it but I would not do this for a tutorial presentation.

Extract from ancient history tutorial presentation:

> In the course of his speech Pericles/Thucydides highlights the attributes of the Athenian way of life. He explains to his audience why Athens is such a great state and demonstrates this greatness through examples of the system of government and contrasts it with Sparta. He also praises the dead for their bravery and glory that they have won in the manner of their death, comforting the parents with the pride that they can have in this. The main part of the speech is an act of self-adulation in which the Athenian system of government is praised and described as:
>
> - unique in the ancient world;
> - a model for other states;
> - reliant on rule of the many, not the few;
> - poverty not a restriction;
> - laws are obeyed;
> - celebrates religious festivities;
> - centre of the world – can get everything;
> - city is open to the world;
> - militarily superior despite no training;
> - doesn't need allies in war;
> - refined city;
> - uses wealth sensibly;
> - citizens participate in public life;
> - discuss before making decisions;
> - generous city hence many friends;
> - educator of Hellas – versatile citizens;
> - worthy to rule others.

Comment

The student wrote up this presentation before the tutorial to use as her notes. Notice how she uses bullet points as a way of focusing on the key issues she is going to talk about.

Example 5: An essay based on an interview

What the student said about this:

> *This was like an essay but it was based on an actual interview I had carried out. What I did was use the things that Andrew had said in the interview and link these to the theoretical things we had been studying on the course. So there were bits of quotes from the interview and then references to reading I had done which seemed relevant to what Andrew had told me about himself and his family in the interview.*

Extract from an essay based on an interview: 'We're all that hotch-potch': Negotiating identities as a Goan in Edinburgh:

> Before discussing identity in depth we first need to discuss what it is. It is an ambiguous term because it involves notions of individuality and collectivity – difference and similarity (Byron 1996: 292; Guibernau and Rex 1997: 4; Jenkins 1996: 3). Each person has an individual unique identity of the self, yet people are identified in terms of groups. For example, Andrew identifies himself as Goan or Indian, as part of a state or a nation, yet he also identifies himself by the culture that he and his wife have created, something that is unique to them. In this sense their identities are multiple.

Comment

Here the student merges together her use of theoretical readings with reference to more empirical interview data. Used together both are crucial to the development of her argument.

Example 6: A seminar paper

Roman historiography: problems and preconditions
What the student said about this:

> *We were given the questions for this seminar paper. We had to address these in the actual seminar presentation and then hand in our written version at the end.*

Extract from seminar paper 'Roman historiography: problems and preconditions':

Were there clear rules for writing history? When do they seem to have first appeared?

The sources appear to imply that there was, by the time of Cicero, a generally accepted way of writing history. Sources 2a and 2b tell us that there must be impartiality in historical writing and Cicero presents this as a 'law of history'. However, looking at the other source materials we can see that this 'law' was not always adhered to and much of Roman history was written in a biased manner, for example in 4a we see Cicero again, but here he is asking Lucceius to 'neglect the laws of history'.

Do Roman historians appear to have gone in for serious research on their material?

There does appear to be research done by Roman historians, but obviously the extent of their research will always depend on the individual. Dionysios of Halikarnassos (3b) tells us that the early historians did not research much, but that the events that were contemporary with them were written from personal experience. We can see that, in contrast, Cicero (3c) seems to be very interested in getting exactly the right chronology and is aware that earlier texts do not always agree.

Comment

This paper was written to help the student to give a seminar presentation in archaeology. In this particular instance she has been asked to make reference to different source material and address specific questions in the presentation. This is rather different from the tutorial paper, above, where she conceptualized her own ideas in bullet points.

Examples 1–6 above all indicate very different kinds of writing, and yet they are all excerpts from actual examples that this student had to tackle as part of her studies. So how did she approach these different writing tasks? Before she could start she needed to get some idea of what the writing was for, what ideas she needed to convey and how best to convey them. She also needed to think about who was going to read her work. The kinds of questions she needed to ask herself were:

- What kind of writing is this: essay, report, collaborative project, seminar paper?
- What is it for: assessment, support for an oral presentation?
- Who is going to read it: tutor/lecturer, other students, me?

Hence she needed to think about:

- Topic: what is this writing about?
- Form: what kind of writing is this?

- Purpose: what is it for?
- Audience: who is going to read it?
- Situation: what is the context in which you are writing this?

In addition we can see that she also had to consider herself as a writer. How much of herself could she put in and how much should she leave out of her writing? So, to the above list we can add:

- Writer: to what extent should the writer's own voice be heard?

Activity Forty-seven: Comparing writing

Now we are going to build upon our student's experiences in order to think about these issues in terms of your own writing. As always it is more productive if you can do this exercise with a colleague. Collect together a number of pieces of your own assessed writing. These do not have to be from your university studies; they may be from school, college or a previous course you have done. Now make a list of what you see as some of the similarities and differences between them. You may want to look back at the examples that we used above and our comments on them.

Now think about each piece of writing in terms of:

- Topic: what is this writing about?
- Form: what kind of writing is this?
- Purpose: what is it for?
- Audience: who is the reader, both real and imagined?
- Situation: what is the context in which you are writing this?
- Writer: how do you include yourself as the writer? Do you use 'I', 'we' or the third person? Do you use the passive voice (e.g. 'it is argued that')?

We are beginning to see how different kinds of writing are essentially different ways of getting things done. This might seem a strange way to think about writing, but all writing has a job of work to do. One of the problems with being a student writer is that there is often some confusion about the job of work that your writing is doing, and this makes writing at university more difficult than it might be in, for example, a work situation.

In Activity Forty-eight, we are concerned with issues of both form and layout. We ask you to think about these because they can tell us a lot about the purpose of the text and the context in which we might expect to find it. Some kinds of writing that you are asked to do at university have very formulaic structures. That is, the way in which they are laid out and the ways in which things are written are quite clearly determined by specific conventions, which should be described and explained by the guidance you receive from your tutor. You will need to check out the guidance that you receive about writing for any particular course. This is because, as we have said before, writing conventions may differ as you move between different disciplines and professions.

Activity Forty-eight: Looking at writing features

Now look at the examples of your own writing again.

- Look at the kind of vocabulary that you have been using. Are similar words and phrases being repeated in the different examples?
- Do you use any graphs, tables, diagrams or symbols?
- Do you use any other kinds of visuals (e.g. photographs, downloaded web pages)?
- Do you use headings?
- Do you use bullet points?
- Do you use a question and answer format?
- Do you use a personal or impersonal style?
- Do you use the passive voice (e.g. 'different layers were laid down in different ways')?

12.2 Report writing

In this section we look in more depth at report writing. Imagine that your tutor has asked you to write a business report for your course. Obviously the only person who is going to read that report is going to be your tutor. In this case, the real purpose of the writing is not 'real' at all, since you are writing the report so that you can get a mark and pass the course. What you have to do in this case is to imagine an audience over and above your tutor. You have to imagine that you are writing for a business audience when, in fact, you are only writing for your tutor. In a real business context it is also quite likely that you would be writing collaboratively with others. In your report for your tutor you may use 'we' as if you had been writing with other people, when for assessment purposes it is only 'you' who actually did the writing. This kind of writing may actually require you to be more imaginative about the intended audience than you would have to be if you were writing a university essay. That is, you need to imagine yourself in the context where a particular kind of writing, like a business report, might be written. This is something you need to take into account when you are asked to undertake this kind of writing. It illustrates how other kinds of writing are rather different from writing a university essay. An essay is usually specifically designed for assessment purposes – the audience is assumed to be the actual reader, the person who will mark your work. In contrast, some of the other types of writing that you do at university, like report writing, are more concerned with communicating with others in a broader professional context. They are designed to mirror similar ways of communicating outside the university. This is why you might find similarities with the kinds of writing people do in professional contexts or in other situations.

A report generally has three main functions:

- to explain *why* something was done;
- to describe *how* it was done;
- to summarize and conclude the outcome of a particular action, or set of actions.

One thing that makes a report distinctive is that it generally has a very clear structure, although this will vary from context to context. A report needs a logical structure to make things very clear to the reader. Detail tends to be more prominent than argument. In this sense, a report is generally more accessible to a reader than an essay, which relies on the development of an argument. A report makes extensive use of subheadings, numbering and lay-out. Another important element is the use of appendices. These generally carry information which is very important but does not fit into the main body of the report.

One thing that makes a report distinctive is that it breaks things up into manageable sections and these are immediately obvious to the reader. This means that the reader can find what they are looking for very easily. This is also why a contents list is important because it tells the reader where to look for particular information.

There are often specific conventions used in report writing. For example, it is common to avoid the use of 'I', and reports are often written in the passive voice. Many reports begin with an 'executive summary', which is similar to an abstract and summarizes the main points of the report in continuous prose. Some of these conventions come from professional bodies and in this case the course guidelines you receive on report writing will address these.

Below we give an example from one university business school of a specific structure for a business studies report.

TITLE PAGE

Report on ....

Prepared by ....

For...

Date..

CONTENTS PAGE

CONTENTS	PAGE
....	....
....	....

1. INTRODUCTION

1.1 Terms of reference

This report is the result of an investigation into complaints made by staff about the internal post service at XYZ. A working party was set up on XX/XX/XX to investigate the nature of these complaints and to make recommendations as appropriate.

1.2 Procedure/methodology

In order to investigate the nature of the complaints the following investigatory procedures were adopted:

1.2.1 questionnaires were sent to all members of staff (*see Appendix A*);
1.2.2 a cross-section of the staff was interviewed (30 in total);
1.2.3 the post room supervisor was interviewed;
1.2.4 the post room staff were interviewed;
1.2.5 the service was monitored for one week.

2. Findings

2.1 The current provisions
2.1.1
2.1.2

2.2 Staff attitudes and expectations
2.2.1
2.2.2
2.2.3

2.3 Post room problems
2.3.1
2.3.2
2.3.3

3. Conclusions

The main conclusions drawn by the working party were as follows:

3.1
3.2
3.3

4. Recommendations
Consideration should be given to the following measures:

4.1
4.2
4.3

Appendix: the questionnaire

THIS IS AN EXAMPLE OF ONE WAY OF WRITING A REPORT. REMEMBER THAT STRUCTURE AND LAYOUT WILL VARY DEPENDING ON THE SUBJECT OF THE REPORT
Reproduced from 'Study Skills and Learning Materials',
University of North London Business School (1995)

Activity Forty-nine: Writing a report

Remember that the format you use for a report will depend very much upon the professional context within which you are writing and the guidance that you receive from your tutor. Now make an outline structure for writing a report based on the guidance that you have received from your department.

12.3 Dissertations and projects

As you approach the end of your studies at university you may well be asked to prepare a long piece of written work such as a dissertation or project. The specific guidance you receive will help you to work out many of the formal features, as projects and dissertations vary according to the subject or discipline, and the two terms may be used interchangeably. In some disciplines a dissertation means a 'long essay', and the only thing that makes it distinctive is its length. You are also likely to be given the freedom to choose your title. In other disciplines or subjects a dissertation is broken up into clearly signalled sections. If this is the case it is common for the work to be preceded by an abstract which provides a useful summary. This means that the reader can see straight away what your dissertation will be about. A dissertation or project may begin with a short review of the relevant literature. If it has involved some of your own research or fieldwork there may be a section on methodology, indicating how you carried out your research. You may also indicate the kinds of research questions that you are addressing and have a separate section on your analysis of the findings. You will generally need to develop your own argument which will be supported both by your own findings and by the literature that you have read and referenced. The specific structure of your dissertation or project is likely to follow any general guidelines that you have been given.

Activity Fifty: Identifying components of your dissertation or project

A familiar dissertation or project outline in social sciences might look like this:

Abstract
Introduction
Literature review
Research questions
Methodology (including methods of data collection and analysis)
Presentation of data
Findings
Analysis
Conclusion

Now make a similar list of what you see as the key components of a dissertation or project that you have been asked to write.

A longer piece of writing can give you much more opportunity to put yourself into your work, and to bring together things in new ways which have not been possible in the shorter assignments you have written throughout your course. You may find that you can choose your area of study for a dissertation or project, and also your own title. This gives you the opportunity to make the work your own and say what you want to say, because you will not be constrained by a title set by your tutor. Because a dissertation or project may allow you to write about a topic that interests you, you will probably need to make time to do other kinds of writing which will help you to explore your thinking and your ideas outside the rather formal structures we have outlined above. In Chapter 13 we consider the use of learning journals and reflective writing in helping you to develop your ideas, which will be particularly useful when you come to prepare longer pieces of work.

12.4 Electronic writing

Having looked at some examples of conventional university writing, we now move on to a very different kind of writing altogether, and something that most students and tutors probably do not even think about as writing at all. We call it 'electronic writing' and even though it may never be assessed, you will probably find it becoming an increasingly important part of your writing.

Email

One of the ways in which you are likely to be communicating with your tutors and lecturers and with other students studying your courses is through email. Your tutor may set up email lists so that they can communicate with all their students on one course at the same time. They may also set up an email list for students to discuss course issues together. You can use these environments to explore your ideas and get feedback from others. They can help you to develop your thinking in much the same way as other kinds of exploratory writing. Even if your tutor does not set up lists to use in this way, you can still work together with other students to help and support each other with your learning, sharing ideas and discussing course issues online. Email exchanges are useful because you can go back and read them at a later date, whereas if you have a face-to-face discussion with a tutor or student you have no permanent record of it, and can easily forget what has been said. Because email creates a permanent record which you can refer to at a later date, it is a valuable medium for exploring course issues with fellow students, and for getting appropriate guidance from your tutor.

Computer conferencing

You may find that your tutor uses computer conferencing as a way of encouraging you and fellow students to work together in groups. This is particularly likely if you are studying at a distance, and do not have the opportunity to meet your fellow students face to face. However, increasingly tutors are also using computer conferencing in face-to-face institutions. It is often set up so that students can work together on a joint project or activity.

Computer conferencing is similar to email but has some added advantages. Once you are placed in a particular group, all the messages you send in that group go to all the members. You always go to the same 'virtual' place to talk to your group, and you will find a record of your discussions in this special space, which is like an electronic seminar group. Computer conferencing systems normally use some kind of 'threading', so that messages on the same topic and with the same message heading will be grouped together. This makes it easy to follow a topic discussion. Depending upon the system in use in your department you may be able to add to your messages hotlinks to web addresses. It is also easy to attach files to your messages so that you can send written or visual texts to everybody who is working on the same activity.

Computer conferencing usually takes place asynchronously – that is, you will be posting and reading messages at different times from your fellow students. This gives you the opportunity to read and respond to messages at a time which is convenient to you. Some universities also make use of synchronous systems so that you can communicate in 'real time', with everybody being online simultaneously. The advantage of asynchronous computer conferencing and email is that you can reflect upon electronic discussions with other students and your tutor, and build these into your own thinking. You have the flexibility to think about your response for some time before posting your own message. You can also edit and refine your message before sending it. You can use these kinds of electronic writing to try out ideas which you may later go on to use in your assignments. This is similar to the use of learning journals, which we discuss in detail in the next chapter.

Electronic writing can help you to:
Try your ideas out by writing about them to and with others.
Be reflective about your ideas.
Get feedback from others.
Prepare for writing your assignments.

The examples we have given here are of sites set up by tutors or the university more generally. You might also like to think about using your own social networking sites to work together with other students.

12.5 Using the Internet as a resource for writing

In Chapter 5 we talked about reading as part of writing. We concentrated on the traditional written texts that you are most likely to use for your studies: books and journal articles. Increasingly, students are turning to the Internet as an additional resource for their studies, and so we approach this section on using the Internet in much the same way as we approached other kinds of reading – that is, in relation to your writing.

When you use reading lists and the library to find the resources you need for completing assignments you can reasonably assume that the resources have been vetted for their authority and validity. Academic staff have decided that certain sources represent authoritative texts for you to read. This is because these books and articles have been written by respected and experienced specialists in the field, whether your studies are in academic, professional or vocational subjects. Unfortunately, you cannot make the same kind of assumptions about resources that you access via the Internet. There are a number of obvious ways in which resources you find using the Internet may be very different from the those you would get from the library. For example:

- they are generally not monitored for their quality;
- they do not give obvious clues about the authority of the text;
- they may be more concerned with presenting an image rather than academic credibility;

- they may include a mix of both written and visual texts;
- they link easily and quickly to other related texts.

We need to make a distinction here between using the Internet to find your own resources and using web-based resources which have been monitored and provided by the lecturers and tutors in your department. You may find that academic staff put resources on the Internet for you to access. These may be lecture notes or other material which has been vetted and sanctioned as appropriate for you to use. Obviously, because they are recommended texts, there is no need to approach them with caution.

When you use the Internet to do your own research you need to develop some understanding of how to evaluate the validity and authority of the sites that you visit. Once you have found a site that you think you might like to refer to in your written work, you need to evaluate it and decide whether you can reasonably regard it as an authoritative source. The next section should help you to do this.

12.6 Evaluating web resources

The URL

URL is short for 'universal resource locator'. It is the address that you type in when you are looking for a particular website. For example, http://www.open.ac.uk will take you to the website of the Open University, UK. If you do not know the URL you can use a search engine like Google, Yahoo or Lycos, to search for the name of the site. The name will usually be displayed with the URL. You can then click on the URL to get to the site.

If you know what to look for, the URL can give you a lot of very useful information about the site and help you to decide whether you can rely on the information it contains. It can tell you whether the site is:

- an academic one: look for the ending .ac.edu
- a commercial one: look for the endings .com or .co
- a charity or non-profit making organization: look for the ending .org
- a government organization: look for the ending .gov

It can also tell you the site's country of origin, for example 'au' applies to sites in Australia.

The publisher

The web address also tells you who published the page. You will find this name after http://www. Look out for web pages which have been published within university websites or the websites of professional organizations. These are likely to be more authoritative than commercial sites for academic purposes.

Personal web pages

Is it a personal web page? Using a search engine to find the personal web page of an author you have been introduced to on your course can be a very good way of finding up-to-date publications by recognized authors. You can sometimes download draft papers from personal web pages.

The author

Who wrote the page? You will often find an email address at the bottom of the page telling you the name of the person who wrote, or is responsible for, the page. When academic staff put resources, course materials and bibliographies on the Internet for their students these can sometimes be accessed by people outside the institution.

Authority and reliability

Does this person seem to be a reliable authority? What organization do they belong to? What have they published? What kinds of sites do the links on the page take you to? Asking questions like these helps you to get a feel for the kind of person who is responsible for a web page. This helps you to make a judgement about whether you should trust the information. People often make links from their own web pages to relevant organizations, groups or discussion lists. Following the links from a web page can often give you some idea about the standing of its author in the wider academic or professional community. Do the links on the page take you forwards or backwards to authoritative bodies? For example, following links to 'Home', which you will normally find on any web page, may take you to the home page of a prestigious university, or to the home page of a commercial company. This will help you to decide how far you can trust this site and how appropriate it is to use it as a resource.

Date

Is the page up to date? You will usually find a date at the end of the page telling you when it was last updated. You need to be careful about using material from pages which have not been updated within the last 12 months. It could be out of date.

Purpose

Why do you think this page was created? What is its purpose? Is it to inform, publicize, explain, add to debates, or is it for marketing purposes? In terms of your research, the former is likely to be more useful – and authoritative – than the latter.

Omissions

What seems to be missing from this website? What do these omissions tell you about the story the author of the website wants to tell? Institutional websites often go to great lengths to present a positive picture of an activity associated with their institution. For example, the website of an academic department might enable you to access pages about some particular research success, but is less likely to take you to pages which offer a critique of that research. You need to be careful about taking things at their face value when you access material and resources on the Internet. They may present a one-sided perspective which will not be very useful when you come to refer to this work in your assignment.

Activity Fifty-one: Evaluating web resources

Use a search engine to find a web resource that you might use in one of your assignments. Now evaluate the site in terms of:

* URL
* Publisher
* Author
* Personal web pages
* Authority and reliability
* Purpose
* Date
* Links to other pages
* Omissions

Would you use this page as a resource in your written work? How would you reference the page? This is a good task to do with another student on your course.

12.7 Visual and written texts

One thing that you might have noticed when you were doing your web searches was the way in which web pages make use of a combination of visual and written material in order to present their message. This is obviously one important way in which web pages differ from more traditional published texts, which often rely rather heavily on the written word. When you come to write your assignments you may also find yourself using a combination of text and visual elements. Look back to the example of collaborative writing in the case study at the beginning of this chapter. The writers relied on photographs to do a lot of the work that one might normally expect writing to do. Because they used a picture of the square they did not need to use the written text to describe the scene in as much detail. The words and the photograph worked together to create the background for the collaborative assignment. When you use visuals you may be able to rely on the visual to do some of the work that writing would normally do, but you cannot necessarily assume that the visual will be immediately obvious to the reader any more than the writing. Verbal and visual elements always work together in a text to enhance understanding.

Notes

- There is no one single way of writing. Remember that you will need to develop your own strategies for tackling different kinds of writing in your courses.
- You can represent your ideas in visual as well as written form in your assignments.
- Electronic writing provides new possibilities for working collaboratively with other students.
- You need to evaluate web resources carefully for their academic suitability.

13

Learning journals and reflective writing

Learning journals • Reflecting on practical work • From journals to reflective essays • The 'learning cycle' and different kinds of writing • A final reflection

Journals make the learning process visible.

It forced me to explore areas I would normally have shut away.

It's good to have a section of work which takes a more relaxed and personal approach to the course.

At the beginning of this book we stressed how writing and learning are part of the same process. Whenever you write you make new knowledge for yourself, which is why no two people ever write even something simple in exactly the same way. As we have explored throughout this book, the process of writing an assignment in all its stages is part of learning the subject you are writing about. In this chapter we look more closely at writing for learning, or *exploratory* writing.

Until now we have been concentrating on the assignment that you hand in to your tutor, the final *product* that they will read and assess. This is a demonstration of what you can say and do at a particular moment. Much of the advice given to students on writing essays starts from the point of view of this end product. In this book we have been trying to combine two approaches: to think about what is required of you for the final product, and to explore the different processes you have to go through in order to get there. To do this we have often suggested that you write brief pieces to help you develop your thinking or practise your writing – to carry out exploratory writing. The purpose of such writing is to help you to learn, and you do not need to think of it as a final product. When you practise writing your knowledge in this way you are also developing your quality of writing, so exploratory writing can help you to learn and to write well. From time to time you may be asked to hand in exploratory writing to your tutor for some feedback. More often though it is something you do just for yourself, or perhaps to share with fellow students, during or outside a teaching session. In this final chapter we will be looking at an extended kind of exploratory writing: the learning journal.

13.1 Learning journals

Learning journals are more elaborate than most exploratory writing and are sometimes formally assessed, which may alter how you approach them. In this chapter we focus on the learning journal as a non-graded, exploratory kind of writing.

Learning journals are a type of writing that give you an overview of a whole course, from beginning to end. If you have to write a learning journal for a number of courses, you will have a record of much of your learning at university, which will help you to bring together the different parts. Learning journals can also be seen as a particular kind of writing, as explored in the last chapter. As one tutor put it: 'journals help to make the learning process visible'.

Learning journals may be kept for different purposes – for example:

- On professional courses, to make links between theoretical and practical work through reflection on experience.
- On academic courses, to help you to make sense of the course ideas and relate them to your own thinking and experience.
- For yourself, as a personal account of your journey through a course, to help your learning and give yourself a record of it.
- To help you make sense of the different kinds of writing you might be required to do at university.
- Occasionally as an assessed part of a course, or as a basis for another kind of assessed work, such as a reflective summary.

What if your learning journal *is* assessed?

Although we are looking at learning journals as a form of exploratory writing, they are sometimes used as an assessed part of a course and will therefore be graded. In this case, you also have to think of the journal as a final product, and the guidelines for it will be more detailed and prescriptive than for a journal written primarily for yourself as a learning tool. Students can find writing a journal for grading causes problems because it is difficult to be genuinely exploratory in your own way while at the same time trying to think about what is expected of you for assessment. At this point the tutor feels to you less like a 'sympathetic' reader and more like a 'judge'. How, for instance, can you say you 'don't understand' when the whole aim of a course is that you should? This is a problem that course designers often acknowledge themselves about learning journals and therefore they may set work for assessment that *relates* to the learning journal rather than formally assess the whole journal directly. For example, one course asks students to draw on their journals in order to write a reflective essay at the end of the course – something students find very difficult to do if they haven't kept their journals up to date! Another course asks students to submit selected extracts from their journals along with a final evaluation of both the journal and their learning on the course. On yet another course the journal has to be submitted along with other coursework but is not itself actually assessed.

Sometimes, however, the journal is assessed directly. If this is the case then you will need to follow any guidelines you are given and check with the tutor, if you can, about any difficulties you may have with what may be an unfamiliar kind of writing. Try not to get anxious about this. In the end, it is probably best for you to keep to the principle that learning journals are intended for you to explore course material and processes in your own way. Tutors want you to be honest and want to see how you have created your own route through the course – this is why they set a learning journal for assessment in the first place. It is therefore a good idea to write your journal on the assumption that the reader is interested in your own learning and ideas.

Activity Fifty-two: Thinking about diaries

There are many different kinds of learning journal but they can all be compared to a personal diary. Most people who have kept a personal diary find that a learning journal is different, because the subject matter and situation is different, but there are also similarities.

Have you ever kept a diary of any kind? Make notes on what it was, why you kept it, who was the intended reader and what you gained from it.

Many students find that keeping some kind of learning journal helps their study, and they also enjoy writing it. We hope that the rest of this chapter will explain why, and give you some ideas about how to write one. If you are on a course that requires you to keep a learning journal, you will probably be given guidelines for it. In this case, you might use this chapter to think more fully about what writing a journal involves. We suggest a number of activities connected with writing learning journals and give examples of what students have written. As you read these examples and try out the activities, use them to build up a picture of what makes learning journals a distinctive form of writing.

Activity Fifty-three: Writing a journal entry

Learning journals usually begin with an account of the student's expectations of a course. Read the following extract from one student's first entry for a course about political theory. Note how the student writes about what she hopes to learn on the course and how she relates this to her own background – her arguments with her brother!

> I am looking forward to this course because I feel power and politics are central issues to social interaction and the way society functions. Whilst studying for the kinship course, it seemed to me essential that you have to bring in the concept of power to be able to discuss both kinship and gender issues ... My oldest brother is an adamant Marxist ... I was always inclined to disagree with my brother's dogmatic approach to Marx, and would try to argue for other theories, although lacking in concrete knowledge. I am looking forward to hearing more about theories of power, such as Weber's and others and hope to expand my knowledge of their works – perhaps in the hope that some day I may be able to win an argument against my brother!

At the beginning of a course or of just one session, write a learning journal entry about what you expect and hope to get out of it, in particular noting any questions that you hope the course or session may answer. Write in sentence form rather than notes. At the end of the course or session go back to this piece of writing to check how your understanding has increased and whether your expectations have been met.

What is a learning journal like?

Although there are many different kinds of learning journal, they all have features in common.

- *A learning journal is written regularly.*
  Most journals are written at least once a week and often more frequently. The regularity is what makes it a 'journal', so that you have a record of what you have been doing and thinking on a course, which you can look back on to see the progress you have made. A journal will rarely be written in note form and is not a substitute for making notes. You may, however, want to extend the notes you have taken from lectures or reading.
- *A learning journal is an account of your progress through a course.*
  When you write a learning journal you are writing about the course as you experience it. You may include accounts of your reading as well as of seminars, lectures and discussions. You may explore your thinking about the ideas and issues raised. You may think about your own learning processes – what you don't understand, and what you gradually come to understand differently. You may write about connections between ideas within the course and ideas outside it; from other courses, the world generally, or your own particular experience. You see from this how a learning journal is about you plus the course, whereas most assignments focus on course material with 'you' as more or less absent (see Chapter 9 for more on your place in your academic writing).
- *A learning journal asks for a different kind of thinking and writing from an essay.*
  A useful way of viewing a learning journal is as an account of your *own thinking* on the page. It is a narrative with you – as 'I' – at the centre. A good deal of a learning journal will be in 'recounting' form (see Chapter 6); that is, you are telling a 'story' about what you have done and how you have felt and thought as a result: 'I did this, I read this'. But you will also include commentary and reflection – your thoughts – about what you did. A journal, then, is altogether more provisional and questioning than an essay, and a more personal document where you can allow yourself to be experimental and to put your own mark on it. Below you will find an extract from the guidelines for a learning journal that was not written every week but consisted of a specific number of entries, each on a different topic. Notice how the tutor stresses the creative aspect and developmental nature of learning journals.

> The entries should be your own personal reflections of what you have read and discussed in the seminar . . . These may be hand-written and do not require the same level of planning as an essay. While it may be appropriate to include lists or spider diagrams, your writing should be mainly in complete sentences. You may decide to experiment with keeping your learning journal as a blog.
>
> Wherever you write it, the idea behind a learning journal is to force you to try to develop your ideas through writing. Writing is a form of creativity which offers more than simply getting down your thoughts. Different possibilities and combinations only become apparent as you start to produce written sentences. Following the ideas and chains of association that

start to appear before you often results in different outcomes to the one anticipated when you first sat down. Practice will give you more and more confidence to sit down and write. In the end it is through writing that you will help to develop your capacity for independent thought and originality.

(*Source*: Nick Hubble, University of Sussex course document for Critical Reading, entitled 'England my England' (2001))

Who is your journal for?

As we have said, the reader you might have in mind for a learning journal may well be yourself. In fact, some people always use a learning journal just for themselves, perhaps drawing on it for more public writing or using it as a place for 'first thoughts'. You may also have in mind a fellow student or tutor, who in this case is concerned with your progress and interested in your ideas, rather than with judging your work. One student said that writing journals is like 'having a conversation with myself', another that it was like writing for 'a good friend', who was always there, ready to listen. On the other hand, if a journal is a required part of a course, a tutor may read it. The reader and the purpose of the journal will affect how you write it.

Different kinds of learning journal: different titles

So far we have been talking about learning journals rather as if they were all the same, looking for what is common in them. In fact, as with all university assignments, tutors use versions of learning journals on their courses for many different purposes, and give a wide range of instructions and suggestions about how to approach them. Tutors also often use different names for them, depending on their purpose. Below are just a few examples. Think about how some of these might fit a course that you do, even if a learning journal is not part of the course requirement. Have you come across others? If so, what do they require?

- A *'study diary'* or *'record of study'* usually asks you to think about the course readings and ideas.
- A *'learning log'* asks you to chart your progress through either a whole course or a particular part of it – for example, a group project. You may have to include procedures, such as accounts of group meetings, and your review of processes – for example, how the group worked together, and how you came to decisions.
- A *'reading response journal'* asks you about your own, personal responses to reading – what you remember and find significant. This is a good way to engage with a text in your own terms before you have to stand back and be critical and analytical about it.

- A *'reflective journal'* may be part of a professional course where you are specifically asked to relate course ideas to your practice in the field – for example, on a work placement.

You will see from the above that a learning journal is a particular type of writing that does a particular job, and you can think of it in this way by using the categories we explored in the last chapter (see Activity Forty-seven). In the activity below we apply these categories to a learning journal and ask you to use these to compare this kind of writing with an essay.

Activity Fifty-four: Comparing a learning journal with an essay

Look back to your response to Activity Forty-seven in the last chapter, comparing different kinds of writing. Compare the following list with the most common essay you have to do. For example, the 'audience' for an assessed essay would be a 'tutor/assessor', whereas for the journal it is a 'sympathetic reader'.

The learning journal as a type of writing

Topic	You plus the course
Form	Reflective narrative, often diary-like
Purpose	To reflect on your progress though your course
Audience	A 'sympathetic reader'
You as the writer	Reflective and 'personal', with 'I' at the centre
Situation	Different courses with different aims and expectations

---

Hand-write or word-process?

Can you word-process a learning journal? There is no reason why you should not. In fact, seeing what you have written immediately, on screen or printed out, can give you the sense that your ideas are forming very quickly. However, many people find that writing a journal is easier to do by hand – that pen or pencil to paper is a more 'direct' way of getting ideas down fast. Many students and their tutors find it practical to have a notebook to hand for all kinds of exploratory writing, including notes, sketches and doodles. You might want to have one so that you can write in it at odd moments, not least during a class. On the other hand, if you have your own computer and can use it any time you want, starting to type can make you feel more 'work-like'. If you have a laptop you might find this is as good as pen and paper for jotting down your thoughts and notes. It is a good idea to try out various ways of recording your journal, to see what suits you best. Some students also enjoy taking care with how they present a learning journal, whether typed or hand-written, using illustrations, cuttings and interesting formats and layouts.

How can learning journals help you to learn?

We have said that writing a learning journal is a good way of helping you to work through course material. Below we look at some of the ways that writing a journal can help you to learn, together with some written quotes from students on their experience.

Keep up with the course timetable

> '*It is a good discipline; it helped me to recall and clarify concerns.*'

First of all, keeping a learning journal helps to ensure that you keep up with the course timetable of reading and other activities, by processing one section before you reach the next. When you write regularly about the ideas and information on a course, you are thinking about the material in your own words. This helps you to understand and remember.

Build up your own 'map' of the course

> '*It opened up a space in which it was possible to make connections between topics and hence write coherently on the course as a whole.*'

By writing your own version of the course, you are gradually building up a 'map' of it. At the beginning you won't know what the whole will look like. However, as you proceed you will notice connections and themes, and by the end you will have a whole picture. Of course, the learning journal may not in fact look very coherent; indeed, it might look quite messy and bitty. You may have to read it over carefully, and look for the main themes and connections; that is, use it as a basis for your course 'map'. All the same, you will have the material there if you need to reconstruct the course for yourself – for example, for an exam, a long essay or a future course.

Make connections with your own experience and thinking

> '*It made me realize the relevance of the course to my own life and it was good that the tutor was interested in this too.*'

Another important feature of learning journals is that, because of the way they are conceived and written, they encourage you to make connections with your own experience and previous knowledge. You can also explore your own values and opinions in relation to the course topics. This can make a course more meaningful for you and therefore help you to feel more motivated and engaged in it.

Tackle difficulties in understanding course material

> *'Suddenly, from nothing, it all started to make sense.'*

Writing a learning journal can help you to deal with course ideas. You might begin by simply stating, 'I don't understand this reading' but then write about the bits you do understand or what it is that you don't understand. Gradually it will make more sense. Here is what a student wrote about how her ideas were beginning to get clearer as she worked on readings and a lecture:

> I felt that my responses to the texts, my understanding emerged as [the lecturer] talked out the key point of the texts. Excited. New ways of thinking about what power is, what it does, where it appears . . . and ways of describing these things.

A learning journal also encourages you to ask questions, which again helps you to slowly build up an understanding of your course. You can see in the three questions below that the student, by asking them of herself, is beginning to clarify ideas and issues.

- Is class still the same whether people act or think in terms of it or not?
- Is power defined by those observing or by those participating/experiencing?
- Do different kinds of power affect different kinds of society?

Make your own sense of the course

> *'It forced me to explore areas I would normally have shut away.'*

The opportunity to make your own sense of a course is probably the most important purpose of a learning journal. It allows you to engage with the course material for yourself and to make your own interpretations. This gives you the opportunity to go more deeply into course ideas in your own way.

Express your own opinions

> *'It is good to have a section of work that takes a more relaxed and personal approach to the coursework.'*

As we explored in Chapter 9, when you write essays it can be very difficult to know when and how to put in your own opinion. By contrast, a learning journal absolutely encourages you to do so. This can be empowering and can help you to be more confident about your own ideas. Be as bold or as tentative as you like. Here is an example, about the book *Bartleby* by Herman Melville (1991).

I really enjoyed reading this book, and I think it was more the style than the content. Melville has a way of drawing the reader into his world by describing those details which make the characters real. What does niggle me though is the 'lack' of detail given to Bartleby. I mean that by the end of the book I had no deep understanding of what motivated him to go for the job, begin work and then simply not do the tasks that were requested of him. I felt after reading this book that I had missed something really important . . . One thing it did highlight for me though was the variety of ways we can interpret the meaning of the word 'death'. It is not always a physical thing.

Rethink ideas

'Looking back at the whole of the course shows a certain evolution, more confidence and a wider understanding of the general ideas.'

Having an opportunity to write a cumulative account of your learning on a course means that your ideas can shift and develop, especially if you keep revisiting parts of it. Writing down such changes also helps you to be self-aware about how your learning is working and evolving. Notice how, in the following passage, the writer shifts in her opinion of *Bartleby* after writing an essay, and as she revisits an earlier entry in her journal.

After writing my essay on *Bartleby* I have found a deeper meaning to the book. I found myself more and more interested in the narrator of the story. His reactions to Bartleby intrigue me. Why could he not take positive steps in dealing with him? I think the story is more about the narrator than I previously thought . . . My feeling is that the narrator almost felt Bartleby's despair but was too afraid to go the next step and address the issue.

Notice too how doing different types of writing gives the student different kinds of opportunities for developing her ideas. By this stage she is able to think about the book in a more complex way than previously.

Develop your own 'voice' and 'identity' as a writer

'I slowly realized that I could make my own structure.'

In Chapter 7 we explored how the university essay is a very particular kind of writing and we asked you to think about the difference between an essay and a learning journal in Activity Fifty-four. In an essay you usually have to 'make an argument' and come to a 'strong' conclusion. Some students find it relatively easy to adopt this stance but others do not. One of the reasons is a lack of confidence; as one student said: 'I'm just not the arguing type.' She may not have quite understood what 'presenting an argument' means but, all the same, it is true that the 'voice' of an essay, its 'I', presents itself as confident and sure of what is being said. We also pointed out that the 'I' of a university essay is often invisible.

Writing a learning journal gives you an opportunity to write in a different style and with a different stance. You are not required to come to a 'conclusion' and can explore in a thoughtful way, using the journal to clarify your ideas. Below is an example of a student using a journal in this way. The writer has already gone some way in sorting out the reading and here is expressing a sense of progress. The journal entry was written quite late in a course, and, although the first sentence indicates that the writer is understanding the material, he goes on to say that only now is he 'getting to grips with the subject'.

> At first the everyday forms of resistance may not appear to be resisting, they are obviously not a revolution, small acts of resistance do not have the goal of total social change but are concerned with matters of local concern, but resistance can become part of a larger struggle ... As the article by Scott has been interesting, clear and thorough, this seminar was useful and finally I feel as though I'm getting to grips with the subject.

Many students use a learning journal to experiment with writing, sometimes in a playful way. The writer of the following extract said that she used her journal to try out different kinds of writing, or different 'voices', as she put it. Notice how she uses quite 'poetic' language.

Nationhood

Reiterating a sense of belonging through everyone doing the same thing, feeling the same thing at the same time. Transcending our mortal selves and remembering ourselves as part of a big group that is like us, that somehow understands us – even if only, or indeed specifically, in the face of adversity. It's assumed that this nation thing is so natural as if it's always been there. Through identifying with this intangible yet tangible community we become part of something big, part of something that gives us an identity and significance that is greater than our little selves (or indeed the frustrating and contradictory lives we lead).

Activity Fifty-five: Keeping a learning journal for one course

You may have been asked to keep some kind of learning journal for one or more of your courses. If you have not been assigned a learning journal, or if you want to try out a different way of keeping one, then we suggest you do so for a week as an experiment. As usual this activity will be more interesting if you work with a fellow student, so that you can discuss how it is going.

- Decide where you will write the journal – for example, in a book or a loose-leaf folder. This will depend on whether you intend to hand-write, word-process, or both.
- Think of the different activities connected with a particular course in the last week. These may include readings, seminars, lectures, discussions and using the Internet.
- Take a reading, lecture or discussion and consider what you remember from it, what difficulties it posed for you and what questions it raised.
- Write as if you are writing a note to yourself or a friend. Remember that the main reason for keeping a learning journal is to assist you in making your own sense of a course.

Commentary

If you keep up writing about a course for a few weeks, you will find it useful to look back at what you have written, and especially at the ways that topics may have been revisited and how your own ideas and understanding are evolving. It is a good idea to write on one side only of your paper and use the blank pages to add notes later on.

13.2 Reflecting on practical work

A practical group project often requires students to keep a learning log or journal. This may have different sections, each written differently. In one example of a small fieldwork project, students first had to keep a record of their meetings and the decisions they made. They then had to write more personally about the experience of carrying out the study. Towards the end of the project they had to *reflect* on what they had learnt, in two ways: first, on how their practical work had helped them to understand more about the theory of fieldwork research that they had learnt at the beginning of the course; second, on what they had learnt about working in a group and how they had each contributed.

Here is one student's thoughts about group work:

> I found the exchange of ideas, particularly at the beginning of the project, very productive. Also improving diplomacy skills – when to push an argument and when to accept someone else's idea instead of my own – was very useful. I did all of my report writing with another member of the group and we discussed what the important issues were and worked them into the text together.

13.3 From journals to reflective essays

Sometimes a learning journal may be the basis for an essay. If you are doing a professional course – for example, in the area of health and social work – you will be required to write essays that bring together theory and practice: to relate what you have learnt from experience in the field to theories that you have learnt on your university-based course. You will need to relate 'doing' to 'book learning'. This produces assignments that are different from the standard essay. The *reflective essay* is a mixture of an academic and a professional approach. On the one hand, you may be expected to bring in your personal experience of what happened in a particular case, while on the other hand, you have to make reference to theory, as if you were writing a standard academic essay. So within one piece of work you have to move between different kinds of writing. The next section is designed to help you break down what is involved in writing a reflective essay. While the task is particularly relevant for professional courses, it may also be useful for any course that contains a practical element, such as a group project or fieldwork.

13.4 The 'learning cycle' and different kinds of writing

Many professional courses make use of what is known as a 'learning cycle' (Kolb 1984). The idea is that on a professional course you can learn in different ways at different stages, through different kinds of activities that are designed to help you to integrate theory and practice. These stages comprise:

1. An actual, *concrete experience* – for example, an interview you have carried out.
2. Your *reflection* on the experience, when you analyse and make sense of the activity for yourself, and think about what you may have learnt from it. For example, did the way you conducted the interview give you the information you needed?
3. *Generalizing*, which involves placing what has happened in a wider framework, typically based on your reading about the subject.
4. *Application and planning* – for example, when you plan an interview you draw on your own experience of what an interview is like and on ideas from reading about different types of interview. You may also draw on an experience of an interview you have already done.

Learning from experience is assumed to involve all of these stages, sometimes sequentially, sometimes together, and not necessarily in the same sequence. For example, you might get taught a theory before engaging in fieldwork and need to return to it later. You might, however, begin with practical work, the 'experience'. Different kinds of learning can take place at each of the stages in the learning cycle and each calls for its own kind of writing.

Activity Fifty-six: Writing and the learning cycle

Take each of the stages in the learning cycle and write in a different way for each, using an example of practice from your course. In these notes we will assume that it is an interview you had to carry out, but you could adapt this for other activities. Write in the following different ways, taking not more than five to ten minutes for each stage.

1 Experiencing

Write a short account of the event as if you are 'in' the experience: what happened and what it felt like. You will need to write this as 'personal narrative', in the first person using 'I'. Don't try to get everything exactly accurate at this point because you are writing as if you yourself are very close to the event and your feelings are also important. This account could well form a part of a learning journal entry.

2 Reflecting

Next put yourself at a distance from the event. You are still writing as 'I' in the first person, but now you look back on the event and consider, 'What does this experience mean for me now?' At this point you might also be trying to analyse what went on in more detail -- for example, by studying transcripts of the interview.

- What was important or particularly relevant about the interview?
- What did it tell you about the person you were interviewing, the situation or the issue?
- What might you have done differently?

3 Generalizing

Writing in the third person, try to think about this event in relation to other ideas and readings. For example, you might write briefly about what two writers have said regarding the social issue that your interview referred to; or maybe about what has been written on the issues associated with conducting such interviews.

- Where does this experience fit?
- What framework can you find to make sense of it?

4 Application and planning

Finally, write some guidance notes to a student on your course about how to conduct interviews, and what issues might arise. This time you will write in the second person, addressing your reader as 'you' and the exercise will further clarify issues about the process for you. You might also want to refer to these notes later for further work.

Now look back at what you have written and (preferably with a friend) consider the following questions:

- What did writing each stage feel like for you, the writer?
- What kind of vocabulary did you use? Did you use a personal or impersonal style?
- Did you use a different kind of 'I' or 'writing self' for each stage?
- What was your sense of the different audience for each piece of writing?
- What have you learnt from doing this exercise?

13.5 A final reflection

Throughout this book we have been asking you to think about how you write and how you learn, and we have stressed the relationship between writing and learning. You learn through the very act of writing, and the more conscious you are of what you are doing when you write, the better you will write *and* learn. We end with an activity that asks you to write a reflective piece about your experience of reading and making use of this guide to writing at university.

Activity Fifty-seven: Reflecting on your experience of this book

Take a few moments to think back over this book. It is unlikely that you have simply read it through from beginning to end, so you may want to choose one particular topic, chapter or approach. Write about your thoughts on what you have chosen, as if writing an entry for a learning journal. Now read over what you have written. Underline three or four words or phrases that seem significant to you. Write about each of these in turn for a few minutes. Now look over what you have written and try to sum up something that you have learnt from the book that you could say to another person.

This activity should help you to start to organize and elaborate your ideas, and to get a sense of what is useful for you in the book at this moment. Thinking back on the whole book should also help you to recall and perhaps reuse some of its ideas. This kind of reflection is typical of the use of learning journals, and the activity is another example of how you can use writing to learn. Whatever type of writing for university you have to do, we hope that the range of ideas and strategies we have suggested will help you to tackle different kinds of assignments with greater confidence and understanding. Remember that writing is an integral part of the process of learning at university. As you develop your understanding of what you have to do, you will find it easier to write for the range of courses and subject areas that you will encounter during your studies. In the process, you will learn to adapt yourself as a writer to writing at university.

Notes

- Writing for learning can be as important as writing for assessment.
- Don't forget, you can keep a learning journal even if it is not a requirement for your course.
- You might like to experiment with keeping your learning journal as a blog.
- Writing a learning journal involves a different kind of thinking from essay or report writing.
- Exploratory writing gives you the space for personal reflections on your academic courses.
- Reflective writing helps you relate theory to practice.

Further reading and some additional sources

If you are looking for additional resources to complement the discussions we have been having in this book, you will probably use the Internet as your first port of call. There is now a plethora of websites which provide guidance on academic writing. As with any resource these vary considerably, both in the depth and quality of the materials available. Many of the sites are linked to writing centres, and, since these tend to be common in the United States, you will find that online writing support is often linked to US universities. Although these are very useful you may need to exercise some caution in making sure that the advice applies to your local context, wherever in the world you are studying. We list below a few sites which we have found useful.

Writing a research paper

http://owl.english.purdue.edu/workshops/hypertext/ResearchW/index.html
This complements the short discussion in Chapter 10 about doing longer project work and writing dissertations. In this instance the focus is on the research paper. These web pages are just a very small part of a much wider, comprehensive and very useful website, from the OWL (Online Writing Lab), Purdue University, USA, dealing with many issues around writing assignments.

Conducting a critical review

http://www.ioe.ac.uk/caplits/writingcentre/criticalreview.1tostart.htm
This complements approaches taken in Chapter 5 on reading but focuses specifically on a critical review of the literature you will use in your studies. It will also help you to write your own critical review and you can do this even if it is not a formal requirement for your assignment. The pages are provided by CAPLITS (Centre for Academic and Professional Literacies) at the Institute of Education, London.

Style Manuals and Writing Guides

http://www.calstatela.edu/library/styleman.htm
Although you will be given guidance on referencing, if you are writing extended pieces of work such as dissertations, you need to make sure that

you follow the accepted conventions for your subject area. This site from California State University, Los Angeles, explores some of these and complements our discussion on referencing in Chapter 8. It might be particularly useful if you are trying to find out about referencing less common citations such as official reports.

Grammar and mechanics

http://owl.english.purdue.edu/owl/
Most people feel that they would like to know more about grammar and punctuation and this site offers a comprehensive overview of these issues.

In addition to these websites, here are a few suggestions for books that we have drawn on, or that go into topics in more depth, or simply that we think you might find useful and enjoy. Details are listed below.

Peter Elbow has been a university teacher of writing in America for many years. He has introduced countless numbers of students and their teachers to the use of 'free writing' that we have adapted as 'practice writing', and have drawn on elsewhere in our book. He first presented the idea in two books where you can find out more about his empowering approach: *Writing without Teachers* (Elbow, 1998) and *Writing with Power* (Elbow, 1998), both originally published in the 1980s. A quite different approach to writing creatively can be found in Mike Sharples *How We Write* (1999). The subtitle of this book is *Writing as Creative Design* which points to his approach to writing as an inventive craft.

Another powerful idea that is an essential part of Peter Elbow's approach is the idea of 'voice', which we look at in several chapters: putting yourself into your writing to let your own sense of you as author and authority come through. One way to explore this is through the notion of 'style' in writing: how you use language to make a particular effect. We haven't directly talked about this because – in talking about different kinds of writing – we have not separated *how* something is written from *what* is said. However, style is something that you might like to think about both in terms of expressing your own 'voice' in a piece, and in terms of communicating clearly with your reader. A good introduction is *Writing with Style* by Rebecca Stott and Simon Avery (2001). The first section is useful for any student, while the second part is probably more relevant to literature students.

The topic of making a persuasive argument, that includes attention to writing style, is treated fully and technically in the study of *rhetoric* that underpins much work on student writing in the USA. A classic and comprehensive text from the 1960s, now in its fourth edition, is *Classical Rhetoric for the Modern Student* by Edward P.J. Corbett and Robert J. Connors (1998).

Many students like to have a book about grammar that they can refer to. A book with plenty of exercises is *Grammar and Writing* edited by Rebecca Stott and Peter Chapman (2001). *The Student's Guide to Writing; Grammar,*

Punctuation and Spelling by John Peck, and Martin Coyle (2005) is a handy and clear reference book.

If you are interested in developing your writing you should have a good dictionary. *The Compact English Dictionary for Students* (2006) has a central insert section on 'Effective Writing for College and Career'. The first section, 'Brush up your writing' relates to using a dictionary and to language usage more generally, while the second section has useful notes about writing that students have to do both for their studies and as they look beyond university to finding a job. The companion *Thesaurus* (2007), which deals with word choice, is a further tool for developing your range and style in writing.

Finally, in recognition of different disciplinary writing there is now a greater emphasis than there has been in the past on materials for students in different fields of study. While many of these are geared towards postgraduate study these may still be useful for undergraduates. One book that is intended for postgraduate social scientists but which is really a classic for all students who are trying to bring together their own approach to writing and what is expected of them at university is Howard Becker's *Writing for Social Scientists* (1986).This is an engaging example of a well-known academic writer in his field drawing on his own practice to help students with examples from his own writing experience. Your own department may produce subject relevant guidelines on how to approach your writing; be sure to make good use of these. You also might try asking your tutors about how they write and you might find their answers to be quite revealing; all writers find writing to be a complex matter even when they are experienced.

References

Allen, T. (1991) War, famine and flight in Sudan 1. Introduction, *Disasters*, 15: 133–6.

Becker, H. (1986) *Writing for Social Scientists*. Chicago: Chicago University Press.

Berkenkotter, C. and Huckin, T. (1995) *Genre Knowledge in Disciplinary Communication: Cognition, Culture and Power*. Hillsdale, Lawrence Erlbaum Associates.

Bose, C. (1982) Technology and changes in the division of labour in the American home, in E. Whitelegg et al. (eds) *The Changing Experience of Women*. Oxford: Martin Robertson/The Open University.

Byron, R. (1996) Introduction, in F. Barth (ed.) *Ethnic Groups and Boundaries: The Social Organization of Culture Difference*. London: Allen & Unwin.

Chang, J. (1993) *Wild Swans: Three Daughters of China*. London: Flamingo.

Compact Oxford English Dictionary for Students (2006) Oxford: Oxford University Press.

Compact Oxford Thesaurus for Students (2007) Oxford: Oxford University Press.

Corbett, E.P.J and Connors, R.J. (1998) *Classical Rhetoric for the Modern Student*. New York: Oxford University Press

Dawes, F.V. (1984) *Not in Front of the Servants: A True Portrait of Upstairs, Downstairs Life*. London: Hutchinson.

Elbow, P. (1998) *Writing without Teachers*. New York: Oxford University Press.

Elbow, P. (1998) *Writing with Power: Techniques for Mastering the Writing Process*. New York: Oxford University Press.

ExChanges: Learning and Teaching at the University of North London (1996) Issue 2. London: Centre for Higher Education and Access Development, University of North London.

Fairclough, N. (1992) *Discourse and Social Change*. London: Polity Press.

González de la Rocha, M. (1994) *The Resources of Poverty: Women and Survival in a Mexican City*. Cambridge, MA: Blackwell.

Goodman, D. and Redclift, M. (1991) *Refashioning Nature: Food, Ecology and Culture*. London: Routledge.

Guiberneau, M. and Rex, J. (1997) Introduction, in M. Guibernau and J. Rex (eds) *The Ethnicity Reader: Nationalism, Multiculturalism and Migration*. Cambridge: Polity Press.

Harrison, S. (1989) The symbolic construction of aggression and war in a Sepik River society, *Man*, 24: 593–9.

Hirsch, P. (1995) Gender negotiations in 19th century women's autobiographical writing, in J. Swindells (ed.) *The Uses of Autobiography*. London: Taylor & Francis.

Jenkins, R. (1996) *Social Identity*. London: Routledge.

Kolb, D.A. (1984) *Experiential Learning: Experience as the Source of Learning and Development*. Englewood Cliffs, NJ: Prentice Hall.

Laurillard, D. (1988) Computers and the emancipation of students, in P. Ramsden (ed.) *Improving Learning: New Perspectives*. London: Kogan Page.

Layton, R., Foley, R.A. and Williams, E. (1991) The transition between hunting and gathering and the specialized husbandry of resources – a socioecological approach, *Current Anthropology*, 32: 255–74.

Melville, H. (1991) *Bartelby, The Scrivener*. New York: Dover Publications.

O'Day, R. (1985) *The Changing Experience of Women*. Milton Keynes: Open University Press.

Peck, J. and Coyle, M. (2005) 2nd edn *The Student's Guide to Writing: Grammar, Punctuation and Spelling*. Hampshire: Palgrave.

Ramsden, P. (ed.) (1988) *Improving Learning: New Perspectives*. London: Kogan Page.

Rowland, S. (2007) Now then, what am I meant to be doing here? *Times Higher Education Supplement*, June 1st, p. 14.

Sharples, M. (1999) *How We Write: Writing as Creative Design*. London: Routledge.

Smithers, A. and Robinson, P. (1995) *Co-educational and Single Sex Schooling*. Manchester: Centre for Education and Employment Research, University of Manchester.

Stott, R. and Avery, S. (eds) (2001) *Writing with Style*. Harlow: Pearson Education Limited.

Stott, R. and Chapman, P. (eds) (2001) *Grammar and Writing*. Harlow: Pearson Education Limited.

Street, B. (1995) *Social Literacies: Critical Approaches to Literacy in Development, Ethnography and Education*. London: Longman.

Svensson, L. and Hogfors, C. (1988) Conceptions as the content of teaching: improving education in mathematics, in P. Ramsden (ed.) *Improving Learning: New Perspectives*. London: Kogan Page.

University of North London Business School (1995) *Study Skills and Learning Materials*. London: University of North London.

West, L. (1988) Implications of recent research for improving secondary school science learning, in P. Ramsden (ed.) *Improving Learning: New Perspectives*. London: Kogan Page.

Whelan, G. (1988) Improving medical students' clinical problem-solving, in P. Ramsden (ed.) *Improving Learning: New Perspectives*. London: Kogan Page.

Index